Christmas
cooking
with kids

Christmas
cooking
with kids

Annie Rigg
photography by Lisa Linder

RYLAND

PETERS

& SMALL

LONDON NEW YORK

Senior designer Megan Smith
Senior editor Céline Hughes
Location research Jess Walton
Head of production Patricia Harrington
Art director Leslie Harrington
Publishing director Alison Starling

Prop stylist Liz Belton
Indexer Penelope Kent

First published in 2010 by
Ryland Peters & Small, Inc.
519 Broadway, 5th Floor,
New York, NY 10012

www.rylandpeters.com

10 9 8 7 6 5 4 3 2 1

For digital editions visit
rylandpeters.com/apps.php

Printed and bound in China

Library of Congress Cataloging-in-Publication Data
Rigg, Annie.
  Christmas cooking with kids / Annie Rigg ; photography by Lisa Linder.
    p. cm.
  Includes index.
  ISBN 978-1-84975-025-7
  1. Christmas cookery--Juvenile literature. I. Title.
  TX739.2.C45R55 2010
  641.5'686--dc22
                    2010020940

Notes
• All spoon measurements are level, unless otherwise specified.
• Ovens should be preheated to the specified temperature. Recipes in this book were tested using a regular oven. If using a convection oven, follow the manufacturer's instructions for adjusting temperatures.
• All eggs are large, unless otherwise specified. Recipes containing raw or partially cooked egg should not be served to the very young, very old, anyone with a compromised immune system, or pregnant women.

• Sterilize preserving jars before use. Wash them in hot, soapy water and rinse in boiling water. Place in a large saucepan and then cover with hot water. With the lid on, bring the water to a boil and continue boiling for 15 minutes. Turn off the heat, then leave the jars in the hot water until just before they are to be filled. Invert the jars onto clean paper towels to dry. Sterilize the lids for 5 minutes, by boiling or according to the manufacturer's instructions. Jars should be filled and sealed while they are still hot.

Dedication
To all Santa's little helpers

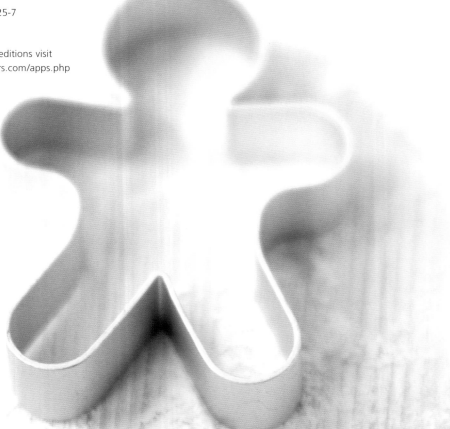

contents

6 *festive fun!*

10 *little treats & gifts*

60 *edible decorations*

78 *cakes & desserts*

100 *party food*

festive fun!

There surely can't be a better time to get children into the kitchen and excited about food and cooking than around Christmastime. Steeped in tradition and distinctive flavors, there's nothing quite like it. At this time of year, everything takes on a magical sparkle and feels that little bit more special, and cooking and eating are no exception.

Most families will have holiday food traditions that have been passed down through the generations—even something as simple as preparing the ingredients for a much-loved pumpkin pie. The simple tasks of weighing and stirring the batter while making wishes is something that everyone, no matter what their age, can get into. Maybe your family makes Sugar

Mice for popping into the bottom of the stockings hanging at the ends of the beds on Christmas Eve, or edible decorations that add something extra special to your festive home. If you always leave a plate of goodies for Santa and his reindeer as they stop off at your house delivering gifts, why not make some delicious iced carrot-shape cookies for Rudolf and his pals, and leave Santa a well earned slab of homemade fruit cake? At this time of year, no special touch goes unnoticed.

Festive cooking doesn't have to mean hours spent in the kitchen measuring and stirring. A batch of Peppermint Creams can be prepared in no time at all and, packed into pretty boxes, these well loved sweet treats make excellent gifts. Just

remember not to leave the confectioners' sugar unattended for too long or the consequences could be very messy, as my mother will tell you. She returned home one day when I was little to discover that my brother and I had taken over the kitchen and turned it into a very sticky snow scene!

At this time of giving and receiving gifts, there is something very special about homemade presents, particularly those that can be eaten. A box of Biscotti or bag of Coconut Ice made with love and tied with a beautiful ribbon are guaranteed to bring joy to all those lucky enough to receive them.

There's something in this book for kids of all ages, for those more confident in the kitchen and those just starting out on an exciting food journey. Marshmallow Snowmen are ideal for little fingers to make as they require no cooking or chopping, and for those a little older who might need less supervision, why not bake

and frost a divine Coconut Cake, complete with beautiful marshmallow peaks?

As this is THE party season, there are loads of dishes that the kids can make to serve to their friends or even to make together for a sleepover. Pigs in Blankets and Cheese Straws are always a big hit at parties with little ones, and if they've had a hand in making them, they'll taste so much better.

There are not only delicious goodies to nibble on, but also plenty of ideas for edible decorations, from the very simple such as making a silver Candy Tree tied with pretty packages and threading popcorn into garlands, to the more labor-intensive such as a Gingerbread House, which would make a show-stopping centerpiece for any Christmas teatime table.

This year, start some new traditions with the children in your family. Give everyone an apron and a wooden spoon and let the fun begin.

basic recipes

This yellow cake recipe can be baked in almost any shape and pan. It can also be used to make cupcakes—just add frosting.

basic yellow cake

medium cake, for a 7-in. round cake pan

1½ sticks unsalted butter, softened

¾ cup plus 2 tablespoons sugar

3 eggs, lightly beaten

1 teaspoon vanilla extract

1⅓ cups all-purpose flour

3 teaspoons baking powder

a pinch of salt

3 tablespoons milk, at room temperature

large cake, for a 9-inch round cake pan

2 sticks unsalted butter, softened

1¼ cups sugar

4 eggs, lightly beaten

1 teaspoon vanilla extract

2 cups all-purpose flour

4 teaspoons baking powder

a pinch of salt

3–4 tablespoons milk, at room temperature

1 Preheat the oven to 350°F. Grease the cake pan you are using.

2 Put the butter and sugar in the bowl of an electric mixer (or use a large bowl and an electric whisk). **Ask an adult to help you** cream them until very pale, light, and fluffy.

3 Gradually add the eggs, mixing well between each addition and scraping down the side of the bowl with a rubber spatula from time to time. Add the vanilla and mix again.

4 Sift together the flour, baking powder, and salt. Add to your mixing bowl and mix again until smooth and well mixed. Add the milk and mix again. Spoon the mixture into the prepared cake pan and spread evenly.

5 **Ask an adult to help you** put the pan on the middle shelf of the preheated oven. Bake until the cake is golden brown, well risen, and a skewer inserted into the middle of the cake comes out clean.

Timings will vary according to the recipe that you are using.

Here are some of the frostings that are used throughout the book. Refer to individual recipes for further instructions.

chocolate glaze

6 oz. bittersweet chocolate, chopped

1 tablespoon safflower oil

1 **Ask an adult to help you** put the chocolate and oil in a heatproof bowl over a pan of barely simmering water or in the microwave on a low setting. Stir very carefully until the chocolate has melted, then let cool for about 10 minutes before using.

glacé icing

2 cups confectioners' sugar

2–3 tablespoons water or lemon juice

1 Sift the confectioners' sugar into a bowl and, using a balloon whisk, gradually stir in enough water or lemon juice to make a smooth icing that will coat the back of a spoon. Add more water or juice for a runnier icing.

chocolate frosting

6 oz. bittersweet chocolate, chopped
1 stick unsalted butter, diced
½ cup milk
1 teaspoon vanilla extract
1¾ cups confectioners' sugar, sifted

1 Ask an adult to help you put the chocolate and butter in a heatproof bowl over a pan of barely simmering water or in the microwave on a low setting. Stir very carefully until melted.

2 Put the milk, vanilla, and sugar in a mixing bowl and whisk until smooth. Pour the melted chocolate mixture into the mixing bowl and stir until smooth and thickened. You may need to leave this somewhere cool for 30 minutes to thicken enough to spread.

buttercream frosting

3 sticks unsalted butter, softened
4½ cups confectioners' sugar, sifted
1 teaspoon vanilla extract (optional)

1 Put the butter in the bowl of an electric mixer (or use a large bowl and an electric whisk). **Ask an adult to help you** cream it until pale and smooth. Gradually add the sugar and beat until pale and smooth.

2 Add the vanilla, if using, and beat again until combined.

9

little treats & gifts

Scrumptious, deep, chocolatey brownies that are topped with a delicious chocolate buttercream and scattered with festive candies.

frosted brownie squares

⅔ cup walnut or pecan
   pieces

1½ sticks unsalted butter

8 oz. bittersweet
   chocolate, chopped

1¼ cups sugar

3 eggs

1 teaspoon vanilla extract

1 cup plus 2 tablespoons
   all-purpose flour

a pinch of salt

Chocolate Frosting (page 9)

red and green candies

edible Christmas sprinkles

*a 9-in. square baking pan,
   greased*

makes 16

1 Preheat the oven to 350°F.

2 Ask an adult to help you line the prepared baking pan with baking parchment.

3 Put the walnuts or pecans on a baking sheet and **ask an adult to help you** put them in the preheated oven. Roast them for 5 minutes, then **ask an adult to help you** remove them from the oven and let them cool.

4 Ask an adult to help you put the butter and chocolate in a heatproof bowl over a pan of simmering water. Stir very carefully until it has melted, then let cool slightly.

5 Put the sugar and eggs in a mixing bowl. **Ask an adult to help you** use an electric whisk to beat until pale and thick.

6 Add the vanilla and chocolate mixture. Mix well.

7 Sift the flour and salt into the mixing bowl and fold in using a large metal spoon or spatula. Add the nuts and stir to combine. Pour the batter into the prepared baking pan.

8 Ask an adult to help you put the pan on the middle shelf of the oven. Bake for about 30 minutes. **Ask an adult to help you** remove the pan from the oven. Let it cool.

9 Spread the Chocolate Frosting evenly over the brownies. Scatter the candies and sprinkles over the top, cut into squares, and serve.

These buns are traditionally served on St Lucy's day in Sweden, December 13th, where they call them "lussekatt." They are normally made into a backward "S" shape, but you could make them into any shape you like. Why not have fun with the dough and make simple animal shapes?

Swedish saffron buns

1 cup milk

a good pinch of saffron
   strands

4–4¾ cups bread flour

1 package (¼ oz.) dry
   yeast

½ teaspoon salt

¼ cup sugar

3 tablespoons unsalted
   butter, softened

⅓ cup sour cream,
   at room temperature

1 egg, lightly beaten

24 raisins

*2 baking sheets, lined with
   baking parchment*

makes 12

1 Ask an adult to help you heat the milk in a small saucepan until hot but not boiling. Drop the saffron strands in and let them infuse in the hot milk for 10 minutes.

2 Tip 4 cups of the flour, the yeast, salt, sugar, butter, and sour cream into a large mixing bowl and stir to mix. Pour the warm milk in and use your hands to mix everything together until you get a dough.

3 To knead the dough, first sprinkle a little flour on a clean work surface. Then shape the dough into a ball and push on it and press it onto the work surface, turning it round often. You'll need to keep doing this until it is silky smooth and elastic—this will take between 4–7 minutes and you may need to add more flour if the dough is too sticky.

4 Shape the dough into a neat ball again. Wash and dry the bowl and sit the dough back in it. Cover tightly with plastic wrap and leave in a warm place until the dough has doubled in size. This can take at least 1 hour.

5 Tip the dough onto the floured work surface and knead for 1 minute. Divide into 12 equal pieces. Roll each piece into an 8-inch long sausage and twist into a backward "S" shape. Place 6 of the buns on one of the baking sheets and the other 6 on the other sheet.

6 Lightly oil a large sheet of plastic wrap, then use it to loosely cover the baking sheets (oiled-side down). Let the buns rise again for a further 30 minutes.

7 Preheat the oven to 375°F.

8 Brush the buns lightly with the beaten egg and push a raisin into each end of the buns. **Ask an adult to help you** put the sheets on the middle shelf of the preheated oven. Bake for about 12–15 minutes, until well risen, shiny, and deep golden brown.

"Lebkuchen" are traditional German Christmas cookies with a good hint of ginger and spices. They can be covered with either a simple white icing or a coating of white or bittersweet chocolate.

Lebkuchen

2 tablespoons honey

2 tablespoons molasses

2½ tablespoons unsalted butter

⅓ cup packed dark brown sugar

grated peel of ½ orange

grated peel of ½ lemon

1¾ cups self-rising flour

½ teaspoon ground cinnamon

2 teaspoons ground ginger

¼ teaspoon grated nutmeg

a pinch of ground cloves

a pinch of salt

⅓ cup ground almonds

1 egg, lightly beaten

Chocolate Glaze (page 8)

Glacé Icing (page 8)

edible silver balls

shaped cookie cutters

2 baking sheets, lined with baking parchment

makes about 30

1 Put the honey, molasses, butter, sugar, and orange and lemon peel in a small saucepan. **Ask an adult to help you** put it over low heat and stir until the butter has melted and everything is well mixed. Carefully remove from the heat and let cool.

2 Sift the flour, spices, and salt together into a mixing bowl, then add the ground almonds. Add the melted butter mixture and the beaten egg and mix until you get a dough.

3 To knead the dough, sprinkle a little flour on a clean work surface. Shape the dough into a ball and push on it and press it onto the work surface, turning it round often. Do this for just a minute or so until smooth, then wrap in plastic wrap and chill in the fridge for at least 4 hours or overnight.

4 When you are ready to bake the Lebkuchen, preheat the oven to 350°F. On the floured work surface, roll the dough out to a thickness of ¼ inch using a rolling pin. Stamp out shapes with your cookie cutters.

5 Place the Lebkuchen on the prepared baking sheets and **ask an adult to help you** put them in the preheated oven. Bake for about 15–20 minutes, or until just begining to brown at the edges.

6 **Ask an adult to help you** remove the Lebkuchen from the oven and transfer to a wire rack to cool.

7 When the Lebkuchen are cold, spread Chocolate Glaze or Glacé Icing over them with a palette knife or back of a spoon. Decorate with silver balls or pipe more glaze or icing over the Lebkuchen with a piping bag. (To make a quick piping bag, take a freezer bag and snip off a corner. Fill with glaze or icing and use to pipe lines onto the Lebkuchen.)

Peppermint creams
are one of the first
things I learned to
make when I was
a child and I still
love making them
now. Once they have
dried out, you can
try dipping them
in melted chocolate
and scattering with
silver sprinkles.
Let dry on baking
parchment before
putting in boxes.

peppermint creams

1¾ cups confectioners' sugar

4–6 tablespoons sweetened condensed milk

½ teaspoon peppermint extract

green food coloring paste (optional)

a mini star-shaped cutter

makes 20–30

1 Sift the confectioners' sugar into a large bowl. Gradually add the condensed milk and peppermint, mixing with a wooden spoon. The mixture should come together like dough and you may need to use your hands towards the end of the mixing.

2 To knead the dough, sprinkle confectioners' sugar on a clean work surface. Shape the dough into a ball and push on it and press it onto the work surface, turning it round often. Do this for just a minute or so until smooth.

3 If you like, you can divide the dough in half and tint one half green using a little of the food coloring. Knead the dough again until it is evenly green.

4 On the work surface, roll the dough out to a thickness of ¼ inch using a rolling pin. Stamp out stars with your cookie cutter and arrange them on a sheet of baking parchment.

5 Let dry out overnight before packing into pretty boxes.

This recipe couldn't be easier or more yummy. Look out for wooden Popsicle sticks in kitchenware or craft stores. Use a variety of edible sprinkles and coatings for your marshmallows. Wrap the finished pops in clear cellophane and tie with a pretty ribbon.

marshmallow pops

5 oz. bittersweet chocolate
5 oz. milk chocolate
5 oz. white chocolate
7 oz. large marshmallows
edible sprinkles, finely
  chopped nuts, and/or
  desiccated coconut

*about 20–25 wooden
  Popsicle sticks*

makes 20–25

1 Chop all the chocolate or break into pieces.

2 Ask an adult to help you put each type of chocolate in a separate heatproof bowl over a pan of simmering water or in the microwave on a low setting. Stir very carefully until it has melted.

3 Push a wooden Popsicle stick through 2 marshmallows. Dip the marshmallows into the melted chocolate (either bittersweet, milk, or white) so that they are evenly coated in chocolate. Use a spoon to help you finish coating the marshmallows and let any excess chocolate drip back into the bowl.

4 Sprinkle the chocolate-coated marshmallows with your sprinkles, chopped nuts, and/or desiccated coconut, then let set on a sheet of baking parchment.

These little Italian cookies are pronounced "reech-ee-a-relly." They're chewy and sticky and yummy. You could add a little more finely grated lemon peel or lemon extract in place of the vanilla if you prefer. Dust them in confectioners' sugar, put them in a pretty box, and give them to your teacher as a present.

ricciarelli

2 egg whites
a pinch of salt
1 cup granulated sugar
grated peel of 1 lemon
½ teaspoon vanilla extract
1 teaspoon almond extract
2 cups ground almonds
4 tablespoons slivered almonds
confectioners' sugar, for dusting

a baking sheet, lined with baking parchment

makes about 20

1 Preheat the oven to 300°F.

2 Place the egg whites in a large, clean mixing bowl with the salt. **Ask an adult to help you** use an electric whisk to beat the egg whites until they're nice and thick. When you turn the whisk off and lift them up slowly, the egg whites should stand in stiff peaks.

3 Gradually add the granulated sugar, whisking constantly until completely incorporated. Add the lemon peel, vanilla, and almond extract and mix again.

4 Fold in the ground almonds using a large metal spoon or spatula.

5 Wet your hands under the faucet, then pull off a bit of the cookie dough, about the size of a walnut, and roll it into a ball. Put it on the baking sheet and flatten slightly. Keep doing this until you have used all the dough.

6 Sprinkle slivered almonds over each cookie.

7 Ask an adult to help you put the baking sheet on the middle shelf of the preheated oven. Bake for about 25 minutes, or until pale gold.

8 Ask an adult to help you remove the baking sheet from the oven. Let the ricciarelli cool, then dust with confectioners' sugar.

marshmallow snowmen

7 oz. large white
   marshmallows
brown writing icing
colored licorice strips
   or fruit leather
chocolate-coated mint
   sticks or pretzel sticks
large chocolate drops
4 oz. white mini-
   marshmallows
confectioners' sugar,
   for dusting

about 10 toothpicks

makes about 10

1 Place the marshmallows on a tray.

2 Push 2 large marshmallows onto each toothpick. **Ask an adult to** trim off any of the toothpick that is poking out of the top.

3 Using the writing icing, pipe dots and lines of icing onto the face to make the eyes, nose, and mouth.

4 Cut the licorice strips or fruit leather into thin strips and carefully tie around the snowman's neck for a scarf.

5 To make the arms, break the chocolate-coated mint sticks in half and push into the sides of the large marshmallow.

6 Pipe a small blob of icing onto the top of the snowman's head and position a large chocolate drop on top. Pipe another blob of icing in the middle of the chocolate drop and stick a mini-marshmallow on the very top.

7 Finally, using the writing icing again, pipe dots down the front of the snowman to look like buttons.

8 Keep making snowmen like this until you have as many as you need to make a fabulous winter wonderland!

9 To serve, scatter confectioners' sugar over the serving dish, arrange the snowmen on top, and dust lightly with more sugar.

This is definitely a recipe for little hands! These cute chaps are such fun to make and look gorgeous on the Christmas table. Why not make one snowman for each person as a place setting?

This is the kind of sweet treat that English grandmothers like to make. Make it a day in advance so that it has a chance to dry out before you cut it into small pieces to serve. This would make an ideal Christmas gift.

coconut ice

14-oz. can sweetened condensed milk
2¼ cups confectioners' sugar
2⅓ cups desiccated coconut

pink food coloring paste

an 8-in. square baking pan, lightly greased

makes 25–30

1 Put the condensed milk and sugar in a bowl and mix with a wooden spoon until smooth. Add the desiccated coconut and keep mixing until well combined—it will get quite stiff!

2 Scoop out half the mixture and place in another mixing bowl. Add a tiny amount of pink food coloring and mix well to color evenly. Add more color if you need to.

3 Spread the pink mixture in the prepared pan and make sure it is smooth and flat on top. Spread the white mixture evenly on top. Cover with plastic wrap and let dry out overnight.

4 Cut into squares, diamonds, or triangles and arrange in a pretty box.

cranberry streusel muffins

1 cup buttermilk

2 eggs

1 teaspoon vanilla extract

2⅔ cups all-purpose flour

1 cup sugar

1 tablespoon baking
   powder

1 teaspoon ground
   cinnamon

a pinch of salt

1 stick unsalted butter,
   chilled and diced

½ cup chopped mixed nuts

2 cups fresh cranberries

grated peel of 1 orange

2 tablespoons unsalted
   butter, melted

*a muffin pan, lined with
   12 paper muffin liners*

makes 12

1 Preheat the oven to 350°F.

2 Put the buttermilk, eggs, and vanilla in a small bowl and whisk lightly.

3 Put the flour, sugar, baking powder, cinnamon, and salt in a large mixing bowl. Add the chilled, diced butter and rub into the dry ingredients using your fingertips. When the mixture looks like bread crumbs, add the chopped nuts and mix to combine. Scoop out about ½ cup of the dry mixture and set aside in a separate bowl.

4 Add the egg mixture to the large bowl and mix until only just combined. Add the cranberries and orange peel and fold in briefly.

5 Spoon the mixture into the muffin liners, filling them almost to the top.

6 Pour the melted butter into the reserved dry ingredients and mix with a fork until crumbly. Scatter evenly over the muffins.

7 Ask an adult to help you put the muffin pan on the middle shelf of the preheated oven. Bake for about 20 minutes or until golden and a wooden skewer inserted into the middle of a muffin comes out clean.

8 Ask an adult to help you remove the muffin pan from the oven. Let cool for 2 minutes, then tip the muffins out onto a wire rack to cool completely.

Muffins are super-easy to make and these ones are full of festive cranberries. You could use fresh blueberries, dried cranberries, or dried cherries if you prefer.

You'll need adult supervision for this recipe when it comes to making the toffee to coat the apples. Look for small, red-skinned apples, which will make the toffee look even more festive. Why not try dipping the bottoms of the toffee apples in sprinkles or finely chopped toasted nuts before putting them on the parchment to set?

toffee apples

8 small apples, eg Jazz, Macoun, or Pink Lady
1½ cups sugar
2 tablespoons corn syrup
juice of ½ lemon
finely chopped mixed nuts and edible sprinkles, for dipping (optional)

8 sturdy wooden skewers or Popsicle sticks

makes 8

1 Wash and thoroughly dry each apple. Carefully push a wooden skewer or Popsicle stick into the stalk end of each apple.

2 Put the sugar, corn syrup, and ²/₃ cup water in a heavy saucepan. **Ask an adult to help you** put it over low heat. Leave until the sugar has completely dissolved.

3 Turn up the heat and simmer until the toffee turns an amber color.

4 Ask an adult to help you remove the pan from the heat. Carefully add the lemon juice —take care as the hot toffee may splutter. Working quickly, dip each apple into the toffee and swirl it around until evenly coated.

5 Let cool for 30 seconds, then dip the bottoms of the apples in mixed nuts or sprinkles, if using. Sit the apples on baking parchment to harden. Serve on the same day.

31

chocolate truffles

3 tablespoons unsalted
butter, softened
⅓ cup packed light brown
sugar
⅔ cup heavy cream
6 oz. bittersweet chocolate

Toppings
5 oz. milk or bittersweet
chocolate, chopped
chocolate sprinkles
cocoa powder
edible silver balls
chopped nuts (hazelnuts
or flaked almonds)

*a baking sheet, lined with
baking parchment*

makes about 20

1 Ask an adult to help you put the butter, sugar, and cream in a saucepan over low heat. Leave until it comes to a boil and the sugar has melted.

2 Break the chocolate into small pieces and tip into a heatproof bowl. Carefully pour the melted butter mixture over the chocolate and stir until the chocolate is melted, smooth, and shiny. Let cool, then cover with plastic wrap and chill in the fridge until it's firm.

3 Making one truffle at a time, scoop a teaspoonful of the chocolate mixture and roll quickly between your hands into a ball. Place on the prepared baking sheet.

4 For the toppings, ask an adult to help you put the chocolate in a heatproof bowl over a pan of simmering water or in the microwave on a low setting. Stir very carefully until it has melted. Let cool slightly.

5 Sprinkle each of your chosen toppings onto a separate plate.

6 Scoop a teaspoonful of the melted chocolate into the palm of your hand and roll one truffle at a time into it to coat completely.

7 Roll in one of the toppings. Repeat with the remaining truffles and let set on the baking sheet before serving or packing into a pretty box.

These truffles make
a delicious gift that you
can make yourself. Choose
between covering them
simply with a dusting
of cocoa or a variety
of nuts and sprinkles.

You will need an adult to help you with this recipe, but it's worth it because it's one that everyone will enjoy eating! Package the fudge into boxes and tie up with fancy ribbons as great gifts.

fudge

¼ cup shelled walnuts
1 stick unsalted butter
¾ cup evaporated milk
2¼ cups sugar
1 teaspoon vanilla extract
1½ oz. bittersweet
    chocolate, chopped
¼ cup raisins

*2 x 6-in. square pans,
    oiled with safflower oil*

makes about 50 chunks

1 Ask an adult to help you put the walnuts in a skillet over medium heat. Toast the nuts for a couple of minutes, until golden, shaking the skillet from time to time so that they don't burn. **Ask an adult to help you** remove the skillet from the heat and chop the nuts.

2 Put the butter, evaporated milk, sugar, vanilla, and 3 tablespoons water in a large, heavy saucepan. **Ask an adult to help you** put it over low heat and stir constantly until the butter has melted and the sugar dissolved.

3 Increase the heat and bring the mixture to a gentle boil. Cook for about 10 minutes. To test if it is ready, **ask an adult to help you** drop half a teaspoon of the hot fudge into a cup of cold water and if it forms a soft ball, it is ready.

4 Ask an adult to help you remove the pan from the heat and, working quickly, divide the fudge between 2 bowls.

5 Drop the chocolate into one of the bowls, allow to melt into the fudge, and stir gently until smooth. Add half the raisins and walnuts, stir, and quickly pour into one pan. Smooth the top with a knife and let set.

6 Beat the vanilla fudge with a wooden spoon until it thickens slightly, add the remaining raisins and walnuts, stir, and pour into the second pan. Smooth the top with a knife and let set.

7 When the fudge is cold, turn it out of the pans onto a board and cut into chunks.

cranberry & pear relish

2½ cups fresh cranberries
1 cup sugar
1 cinnamon stick
1 teaspoon ground ginger
grated peel and freshly
   squeezed juice of
   1 orange
4 ripe pears

*3 small sterilized jars
(see page 4)*

makes about 3 jars

1 Put the cranberries, ²/₃ cup water, the sugar, cinnamon stick, ground ginger, and orange peel and juice into a large saucepan. **Ask an adult to help you** put it over medium heat. Cook until the cranberries have softened and burst, then simmer for another 5 minutes.

2 Peel the pears, cut into quarters, and remove the cores. Chop the pears into small pieces and add to the pan.

3 Cook for a further 15–20 minutes until the pears are soft and the sauce has thickened.

4 Ask an adult to help you remove the pan from the heat. Carefully fish out the cinnamon stick. Taste the sauce and add a little more sugar if needed.

5 Spoon the relish into the sterilized jars, let cool, then cover with the sterilized lids. Store in the fridge until needed.

This is the perfect Christmas relish, as it goes well with baked ham or roast turkey. Why not tie the jars up with labels and ribbons and give away as gifts? Keep the relish in the fridge for up to 2 weeks.

These little nutty cookies look like silvery moons with their dusting of confectioners' sugar. This recipe uses almonds, but you could use chopped mixed nuts instead— simply grind them in the food processor before adding to the mixture. Look for the bags of ready-chopped mixed nuts in the baking section of the supermarket.

almond crescents

⅔ cup confectioners'
  sugar, plus extra for
  dusting
14 tablespoons unsalted
  butter, softened
1 egg yolk
1 teaspoon vanilla extract
2⅓ cups all-purpose flour
1 teaspoon baking powder
⅔ cup ground almonds,
  hazelnuts, or mixed nuts

2 baking sheets, lined with
  baking parchment

makes about 24

1 Put the confectioners' sugar, butter, egg yolk, and vanilla in the bowl of an electric mixer (or use a large bowl and an electric whisk). **Ask an adult to help you** cream the ingredients until smooth and light.

2 Add the flour, baking powder, and ground nuts and mix until the dough comes together into a ball. Flatten into a disc, cover with plastic wrap, and chill in the fridge for 1 hour, or until firm.

3 Preheat the oven to 350°F.

4 Break off a walnut-sized piece of the cookie dough and roll into a short, fat sausage shape in your hands. Bend into a crescent and place on one of the prepared baking sheets.

5 Repeat with the remaining dough, spacing the cookies well apart on the sheets.

6 Ask an adult to help you put the sheets on the middle shelf of the preheated oven. Bake for about 12 minutes or until golden.

7 Ask an adult to help you remove the sheets from the oven. Let cool for 2 minutes, then dust with plenty of confectioners' sugar. Let cool completely before serving.

iced Christmas tree cookies

15 tablespoons unsalted
   butter, softened
1 cup sugar
1 egg, lightly beaten
½ teaspoon vanilla extract
a pinch of salt
3½ cups all-purpose flour
Glacé Icing (page 8)
assorted colored writing
   icing tubes
sugar balls and edible
   sprinkles

*assorted Christmas tree
   cookie cutters*

*2 baking sheets, lined with
   baking parchment*

*makes 12–16, depending
on size*

1 Put the butter and sugar in the bowl of an electric mixer fitted with the paddle attachment (or use a large bowl and an electric whisk). **Ask an adult to help you** cream them until pale and fluffy. Add the beaten egg, vanilla, and salt and mix again.

2 Gradually add the flour and mix until incorporated and smooth. Tip the dough out onto the work surface, flatten into a disc, cover with plastic wrap, and chill for a couple of hours until firm.

3 Sprinkle a little flour on a clean work surface. Using a rolling pin, roll out the dough to a thickness of about ⅛ inch. Stamp out shapes with the cookie cutters and arrange on the prepared baking sheets. Gather up any scraps of cookie dough, knead very lightly to bring together into a ball, and roll out again to stamp out more cookies. Chill in the fridge for a further 15 minutes.

4 Preheat the oven to 350°F.

5 Ask an adult to help you put the baking sheets on the middle shelf of the preheated oven. Bake for about 10–12 minutes until pale golden and firm to the touch.

6 Ask an adult to help you remove the sheets from the oven. Let the cookies cool on the baking sheets before transferring to a wire rack to cool completely.

7 When the cookies are cold, use a small palette knife to carefully spread the Glacé Icing over each cookie, trying to keep it as neat as possible. Use the writing icing tubes to pipe tinsel across each cookie. Position the sugar balls and edible sprinkles over the top to look like tree ornaments.

8 Let the icing set before serving.

Treat these simple Christmas tree cookies like your own blank canvas to draw any decorative design that you like. Look for colorful edible sprinkles and writing icing pens at the supermarket to help you embellish them.

This is a popular Christmas cookie that can either be made the traditional way—in a circle—and cut into wedges, or in a rectangle and then cut into fingers. You could always flavor the basic shortbread dough with lemon peel or even some stem ginger, if you like.

shortbread

1⅓ cups all-purpose flour
3 tablespoons rice flour,
   fine semolina, or
   cornstarch
⅓ cup sugar, plus extra
   for sprinkling
a pinch of salt
1½ sticks unsalted butter,
   chilled and diced

*a baking sheet, lined with
   baking parchment*

makes 8 wedges

1 Sift the flour, rice flour, sugar, and salt into a large mixing bowl. Add the chilled butter and rub in with your fingertips until you get a ball of dough.

2 Sprinkle a little flour on a clean work surface. Tip the dough out of the bowl and onto the work surface. Press or roll the dough into a circle about 8 inches across. Alternatively, you can flatten the dough into a rough rectangle.

3 Carefully lift the shortbread dough onto the middle of the prepared baking sheet.

4 Working your way around the edge of the circle, press the dough between your thumb and forefinger to create a crinkled border.

5 Using a knife, mark 8 wedges into the shortbread, but don't cut all the way through.

6 Chill the shortbread dough in the fridge for 30 minutes.

7 Preheat the oven to 300°F.

8 Prick the shortbread all over with a fork and sprinkle with more sugar. **Ask an adult to help you** put the baking sheet on the middle shelf of the preheated oven. Bake for about 45–50 minutes until light golden.

9 Ask an adult to help you remove the sheet from the oven. Let the shortbread cool a little before cutting into wedges, following the marks you made before baking.

43

Serve these yummy bars with a good scoop of the very best vanilla ice cream or pop into your lunchbox for a special treat.

pecan, toffee, & chocolate squares

1 cup all-purpose flour
⅓ cup confectioners' sugar
1 stick unsalted butter,
   chilled and diced
1 egg white

Topping
3 tablespoons unsalted
   butter
¾ cup packed light brown
   sugar
3 eggs
1 teaspoon vanilla extract
¾ cup pure maple syrup
⅔ cup bittersweet
   chocolate chips
1⅓ cups pecan pieces

*an 8-in. square baking pan
(2 in. deep), greased*

makes 16

1 Preheat the oven to 350°F.

2 Ask an adult to help you put the flour, sugar, and butter into a food processor. Using the pulse button, process until the mixture just starts to come together in clumps. Tip the mixture into the prepared baking pan and pat evenly over the bottom of the pan.

3 Ask an adult to help you put the baking pan on the middle shelf of the preheated oven. Bake for 20 minutes, or until just lightly golden.

4 Ask an adult to help you remove the pan from the oven. Using a pastry brush, carefully brush the top of the bars with the egg white and return to the oven for a further 2 minutes.

5 Ask an adult to help you remove the pan from the oven and let cool. Keep the oven on.

6 Meanwhile, to make the topping, ask an adult to help you melt the butter in a small saucepan over low heat or in the microwave on a low setting.

7 In a small mixing bowl, whisk together the sugar, eggs, vanilla, maple syrup, and butter with a balloon whisk.

8 Scatter the chocolate chips and pecans evenly over the cooled bar base. Pour the filling on top. Ask an adult to help you put the baking pan on the middle shelf of the preheated oven. Bake for a further 35 minutes, or until the topping has set.

9 Ask an adult to help you remove the pan from the oven and let it cool completely in the pan before cutting into squares to serve.

You could add some finely grated lemon peel or lemon extract in place of the vanilla if you prefer in these little French cakes. You do need a special madeleine pan for this recipe—there really is no other way to cook these delicate treats.

madeleines

7 tablespoons unsalted butter

½ cup sugar

2 eggs

1 teaspoon vanilla extract

¾ cup all-purpose flour, plus extra for dusting

½ teaspoon baking powder

a pinch of salt

a madeleine pan

makes about 24

1 Preheat the oven to 375°F.

2 Ask an adult to help you melt the butter in a saucepan over low heat or in the microwave on a low setting. Use some of the melted butter to brush the holes in the madeleine pan so that they are lightly greased. Dust the holes with flour and shake off any excess.

3 Put the sugar and eggs in the bowl of an electric mixer fitted with the whisk attachment (or use a large bowl and an electric whisk). **Ask an adult to help you** whisk on medium speed until the mixture has doubled in volume and is very pale and light.

4 Add the vanilla. Sift the flour, baking powder, and salt into the bowl and fold gently into the egg mixture using a large metal spoon.

5 Fold in the remaining melted butter.

6 Spoon the mixture into the holes in the madeleine pan, filling them to just below the tops. You may need to bake the madeleines in 2 batches if your pan isn't big enough.

7 Ask an adult to help you put the pan on the middle shelf of the preheated oven. Bake for about 10 minutes or until golden brown and well risen.

8 Ask an adult to help you remove the pan from the oven. Let cool in the pan for a minute, then turn the pan upside down and tap on the surface so that the madeleines drop out. Let cool completely on a wire rack, then dust with confectioners' sugar, if you like.

Biscotti are a traditional Italian cookie and are very easy to make. The word "biscotti" means "twice baked." These are made with pistachios and dried cranberries, but you could also use dried figs, raisins, and other nuts, such as almonds or hazelnuts. They are delicious with a glass of cold milk.

biscotti with pistachios & cranberries

3 tablespoons unsalted
   butter
1¾ cups all-purpose flour
¾ cup sugar
a pinch of salt
½ teaspoon baking
   powder
½ cup shelled pistachios,
   roughly chopped
½ cup dried cranberries
grated peel of ½ lemon
1 whole egg
1 yolk
1 teaspoon vanilla extract

2 baking sheets

makes about 20

1 Preheat the oven to 350°F and line one baking sheet with baking parchment.

2 Ask an adult to help you melt the butter in a small saucepan over low heat or in the microwave on a low setting.

3 Tip the flour, sugar, salt, and baking powder into a large mixing bowl. Add the pistachios, cranberries, and lemon peel and mix well.

4 In a separate bowl, whisk the egg, egg yolk, vanilla, and butter with a balloon whisk.

5 Make a hole like a well in the middle of the large bowl of dry ingredients and pour the egg and butter mixture into it. Stir with a wooden spoon until the ingredients are thoroughly mixed and have come together into a ball. Divide the dough into 2 equal pieces.

6 Sprinkle a little flour on a clean work surface. Using your hands, roll each piece of dough into a fat sausage about 8 inches long. Put the logs on the lined baking sheet, leaving plenty of space between them.

7 Ask an adult to help you put the sheet on the middle shelf of the preheated oven. Bake for about 35–45 minutes until golden brown and firm to the touch.

8 Ask an adult to help you remove the sheet from the oven and let cool for 45 minutes. Turn the oven off.

9 When the logs are cold, preheat the oven to 325°F and line 2 baking sheets with more baking parchment.

10 Ask an adult to help you to slice the logs diagonally into ⅜-inch thick slices using a sharp knife. Arrange them in a single layer on the baking sheets.

11 Ask an adult to help you put the sheets on the middle shelf of the preheated oven. Bake for about 20 minutes, or until crisp. You may need to swap the sheets over and turn the biscotti halfway through cooking. Let the biscotti cool before serving.

These are filled with a sugary cinnamon butter and topped with a crazy drizzle of icing. Add chocolate chips to the filling for an extra helping of sweetness!

cinnamon sticky buns

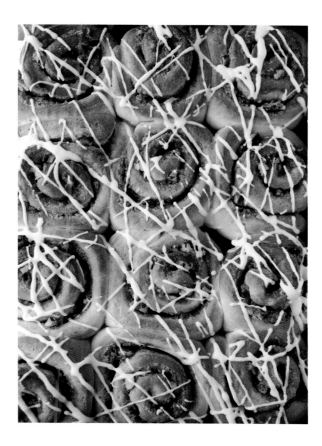

2/3 cup milk

4–4 3/4 cups bread flour

1 package (1/4 oz.) dry
   yeast

a large pinch of salt

1/4 cup sugar

2 eggs, lightly beaten

5 tablespoons unsalted
   butter, softened

Glacé Icing (page 8)

Filling

6 tablespoons unsalted
   butter, softened

1/2 cup packed light brown
   sugar

3 teaspoons ground
   cinnamon

1/2 cup pecan pieces

*a 9 x 12-in. baking pan,
   greased*

makes 12

1 Ask an adult to help you heat the milk in a small saucepan until hot but not boiling.

2 Sift 4 cups of the flour into a large mixing bowl and stir in the yeast, salt, and sugar. Make a hole like a well in the middle and pour in the milk, eggs, and butter. Stir until mixed.

3 To knead the dough, sprinkle a little flour on a clean work surface. Shape the dough into a ball and push on it and press it onto the work surface, turning it round often. You'll need to keep doing this until it is silky smooth and elastic—about 5 minutes—and you may need to add more flour if the dough is too sticky.

4 Shape the dough into a neat ball again. Wash and dry the mixing bowl and sit the dough back in it. Cover tightly with plastic wrap and set aside in a warm place until the dough has doubled in size—about 1 1/2 hours.

5 While the dough is rising, make the filling. Put the butter, sugar, cinnamon, and pecans in a bowl. Beat with a wooden spoon until mixed.

6 Tip the dough onto the floured work surface and knead lightly for 1 minute. Roll and press it into a rectangle about 12 x 20 inches, with a long side nearest you.

7 Spread the filling over the dough, leaving a border of about 1/2 inch around the edges.

8 Starting with the side closest to you, roll the dough up evenly and firmly, but not too tight. Cut into 12 slices and place cut-side up in the baking pan. Lightly oil a sheet of plastic wrap, then use it to loosely cover the baking pan (oiled-side down). Set aside in a warm place for 30 minutes, or until risen.

9 Preheat the oven to 350°F.

10 Ask an adult to help you put the pan on the middle shelf of the preheated oven. Bake for 30–35 minutes until golden brown.

11 Ask an adult to help you remove the pan from the oven. Let cool completely.

12 Using a spoon, drizzle the Glacé Icing over the buns. Let set before tipping them out of the pan and pulling them apart, to serve.

rocky road fridge cake

⅔ cup mixed nuts (eg
  hazelnuts, almonds,
  pecans, walnuts)
14 oz. bittersweet or milk
  chocolate, chopped
3 tablespoons unsalted
  butter
1 tablespoon honey
8 oz. mixed dried fruit
  (eg glacé cherries, figs,
  apricots, raisins)
2½ oz. graham crackers

*an 8-in. square baking
  pan, lined with baking
  parchment*

makes 16

1 Ask an adult to help you put the nuts in a skillet over medium heat. Toast the nuts for a couple of minutes, until golden, shaking the skillet from time to time so that they don't burn. **Ask an adult to help you** remove the skillet from the heat and chop the nuts.

2 Ask an adult to help you put the chocolate, butter, and honey in a heatproof bowl over a pan of simmering water or in the microwave on a low setting. Stir very carefully until melted. Let cool slightly.

3 Halve the glacé cherries and roughly chop the figs and apricots. Break the crackers into small pieces.

4 Add the toasted nuts, dried fruit, and crackers to the melted chocolate mixture and stir with a wooden spoon until combined. Spoon into the prepared pan and spread evenly. Let cool, then cover lightly with plastic wrap and chill in the fridge until set.

5 Cut into 16 squares and serve.

Everyone loves chocolate fridge cake and there is no end to the variety of bits and pieces you can put in it. Choose from your favorite dried fruit and nuts, and maybe add some mini-marshmallows if the mood takes you.

These pretty snowflakes are simply made from a basic meringue, but add a festive touch with a sprinkling of edible silver glitter or silver balls.

meringue snowflakes

¾ cup sugar

2½ oz. egg whites (about 2 medium egg whites)

edible silver glitter

edible silver balls

a piping bag, fitted with a star tip

2 baking sheets, lined with baking parchment

makes about 12

1 Preheat the oven to 400°F.

2 Tip the sugar into a small roasting pan. **Ask an adult to help you** put it in the preheated oven for about 5 minutes until hot to the touch—be careful not to burn your fingers!

3 Turn the oven down to 225°F.

4 Place the egg whites in a large, clean mixing bowl or in the bowl of an electric mixer. **Ask an adult to help you** to beat the egg whites (with an electric whisk, if necessary) until they're frothy.

5 Tip the hot sugar onto the egg whites in one go and continue to whisk on high speed for about 5 minutes until the meringue mixture is very stiff, white, and cold.

6 Spoon the meringue mixture into the prepared piping bag. Pipe little blobs of meringue onto the prepared baking sheets in the shape of snowflakes. Scatter silver glitter or silver balls over the top.

7 **Ask an adult to help you** put the sheets in the preheated oven. Bake for about 45 minutes or until crisp and dry. Turn off the oven, leave the door closed and let the snowflakes cool down completely inside the oven.

goodies for Santa & Rudolf

uncooked batter for Easy
    Fruitcake (page 94)
uncooked dough for
    Gingerbread Shooting
    Stars (page 70)
1¾ cups royal icing sugar
green good coloring paste
orange food coloring
    paste
¼ cup apricot jam
4 oz. natural marzipan
5 oz. white ready-to-use
    fondant or royal icing
Christmas sprinkles

*8 mini loaf pans, greased
    and baselined with
    greased baking
    parchment*

*a carrot-shaped cookie
    cutter*

*a baking sheet, lined with
    baking parchment*

a mini star-shaped cutter

makes lots!

1 Preheat the oven to 350°F.

2 Prepare the Easy Fruitcake as described on page 94. Divide the mixture between the prepared loaf pans, filling them just over two-thirds full. Arrange them on a baking sheet and **ask an adult to help you** put it on the middle shelf of the preheated oven. Bake for about 30 minutes, or until golden brown, well risen, and a skewer inserted into the middle of the cakes comes out clean.

3 Ask an adult to help you remove the sheet from the oven and let the cakes cool for 10 minutes before tipping them out onto a wire rack to cool completely.

4 Prepare the gingerbread dough as described on page 70 and let it rest in the fridge for a couple of hours, or until firm.

5 Sprinkle a little flour on a clean work surface. Using a rolling pin, roll out the dough to a thickness of about ¹⁄₁₆ inch. Stamp out carrot shapes with the cookie cutter and arrange on the prepared baking sheet. Gather up any scraps of dough, knead very lightly to bring together into a ball, and roll out again to stamp out more cookies.

6 Ask an adult to help you put the sheet on the middle shelf of the preheated oven. Bake for about 12 minutes, or until firm.

7 Let the cookies cool on the baking sheets for about 5 minutes before transferring to a wire rack to cool completely.

8 When the cookies are cold, use the royal icing sugar to make up the icing according to the manufacturer's instructions. Tint a quarter of the icing green using the food coloring paste. Tint the remaining icing orange.

9 Ice the cookies to look like carrots using the colored royal icing and spreading it evenly with a small palette knife. Let dry completely before serving.

10 To decorate the cakes, **ask an adult to help you** put the apricot jam in a small saucepan over low heat. Leave until runny, then strain. Brush the top of each cake with a thin layer of the jam.

11 Lightly dust the work surface with confectioners' sugar and roll out the marzipan until it is no more than ¹⁄₁₆ inch thick. Using the bottom of a mini loaf pan as a guide, cut out 8 rectangles from the marzipan and lay one rectangle on top of each cake.

12 Repeat step 11 with the fondant icing and stick the rectangles on top of the marzipan with a little boiled water. Use the star-shaped cutter to stamp out stars. Dab the bottom of each star with water and stick onto the top of each cake. Very lightly brush the stars with a little more water and scatter Christmas sprinkles over the top. Set aside to dry.

13 On Christmas Eve, arrange your choice of goodies on a tray, eg a bowl of popcorn, a few sweets, a clementine, and a glass of milk.

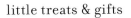

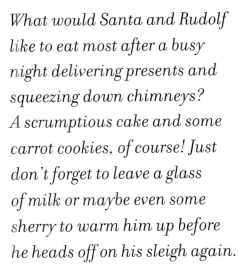

What would Santa and Rudolf like to eat most after a busy night delivering presents and squeezing down chimneys? A scrumptious cake and some carrot cookies, of course! Just don't forget to leave a glass of milk or maybe even some sherry to warm him up before he heads off on his sleigh again.

Topped with a pastry star and filled with cinnamon-spiced apples and cranberries, these little pies are a delicious alternative to plain apple pie. Use storebought sweet tart dough to make them in no time at all!

apple & cranberry pies

2 cooking apples

2 red eating apples

12 oz. ready-made sweet tart dough

¼ cup sugar, plus extra for sprinkling

½ teaspoon ground cinnamon, plus extra for sprinkling

juice of ½ lemon

⅓ cup dried cranberries

1 tablespoon milk

a 12-hole tartlet pan

a fluted round cookie cutter, just bigger than the tartlet pan holes

a star-shaped cutter

makes 9–12

1 Peel both types of apple, cut into quarters, and remove the cores. Chop the apples into small pieces and tip into a medium saucepan. Add the sugar, cinnamon, lemon juice, and cranberries. **Ask an adult to help you** put the pan over low-medium heat, stirring from time to time until the apples are tender.

2 Ask an adult to help you remove the pan from the heat. Taste and add a little more sugar if needed. Set aside until cold.

3 Preheat the oven to 350°F.

4 Sprinkle a little flour on a clean work surface. Roll out the dough to a thickness of about ⅛ inch. Use the fluted cookie cutter to stamp out rounds. Gently press the pastry rounds into the pan holes.

5 Divide the cooled fruit mixture between the pies, filling them almost to the top.

6 Gather up any scraps of dough, knead very lightly to bring together into a ball and roll out again. Use the star-shaped cutter to stamp out stars for the pie tops.

7 Lightly brush the edges of each pie with milk and top with a pastry star. Brush the top of each star with milk and dust with sugar and a little ground cinnamon.

8 Ask an adult to help you put the pan on the middle shelf of the preheated oven. Bake for about 25 minutes, or until the pastry is golden brown and the fruit filling is bubbling.

9 Ask an adult to help you remove the pan from the oven. Let cool, then dust with confectioners' sugar, if you like.

edible decorations

Once you have decided which animal or shape to do, you can color your marzipan accordingly. Use the figures to decorate the Christmas table or even a cake.

marzipan Christmas figures

6½ oz. natural marzipan
assorted food coloring
pastes

makes roughly 10 figures

to make one reindeer

1 Break off 4 walnut-sized pieces of marzipan from the block. Add a tiny bit of red food coloring to one piece and knead it until all the color is evenly mixed in. Repeat to tint the other pieces yellow and black. Leave the fourth piece white. Cover with plastic wrap.

2 Break off another piece of marzipan the size of a small tangerine and tint it brown. Break off a piece of this slightly smaller than a walnut and roll into a ball. Break off another piece the size of a cherry tomato and roll into a ball. Stick it onto the larger piece, slightly forward, for the head. Roll 6 small nuggets of brown marzipan into balls. Flatten 2 of them and stick to the head for the ears. Attach the remaining 4 around the body for legs.

3 Roll a small nugget of red marzipan into a ball and attach to the face for the nose.

4 To make the eyes, break off 2 tiny pieces of white marzipan, roll into balls, and flatten into discs. Roll 2 smaller balls of black marzipan into discs and stick in the middle of the white discs. Attach the eyes to the reindeer's face.

5 Finally, break off 2 small nuggets of yellow marzipan and shape roughly into antlers. Attach to the top of the head.

to make one snowman

1 Break off a small walnut-sized piece of marzipan from the block and tint it red using the food coloring paste. Take a slightly smaller piece of marzipan and tint it black. Tint another tiny piece orange. Cover with plastic wrap.

2 Break off another piece of marzipan the size of a small tangerine. Divide this in 2—one piece slightly larger than the other. Roll both into balls and put the larger one on the work surface for the body. Stick the smaller ball on top for the head.

3 Roll the red marzipan into a thin snake and wrap this carefully around the snowman's neck for a scarf.

4 To make the eyes and buttons, break off 4 tiny pieces of black marzipan. Roll into balls and stick 2 of each onto the face and body.

5 Roll the orange marzipan into a carrot shape for the nose. Stick this in the middle of the snowman's face.

to make one penguin

1 Break off a tiny piece of marzipan and tint it orange using the food coloring paste. Break off a tangerine-sized piece of marzipan from the block and tint it black. Break off a walnut-sized piece and leave it white. Cover with plastic wrap.

2 Break off a cherry tomato-sized piece of black marzipan and roll into a ball for the penguin's head.

3 Reserve a tiny amount of white marzipan for the eyes. Roll the rest into a ball and put on the work surface for the body. Stick the black ball on top for the head.

4 Take a piece of the remaining black marzipan and flatten into a disc about the same width as the penguin's body and stick it onto the back of the penguin.

5 Take 2 smaller pieces of black marzipan and shape into wing shapes. Attach to the side of the body.

6 For the feet, take 2 small nuggets of black marzipan, roll into balls, and flatten into oval discs. Press onto the bottom of the penguin's body so that they are clearly visible.

7 To make the eyes, take the reserved white marzipan, roll into 2 tiny balls, and flatten into discs. Roll 2 smaller balls of black marzipan into discs and stick in the middle of the white discs. Attach the eyes to the penguin's face.

8 Roll and pinch the orange marzipan into a beak shape. Stick this onto the penguin's face.

Make these little mice at least one day before you want to serve them to give them plenty of time to dry out. The recipe makes enough for a large family of mice—one for each of your family and friends.

sugar mice

2 teaspoons meringue powder
1 teaspoon lemon juice
3–4 cups confectioners' sugar, sifted
pink food coloring paste
small chocolate sprinkles

kitchen twine

a baking sheet, lined with baking parchment

makes 12

1 Put the meringue powder and 2 tablespoons warm water in a bowl. Whisk with a balloon whisk until well mixed. Stir in the lemon juice.

2 Gradually add the confectioners' sugar and stir in until the mixture is really stiff—similar to dough. It may be easier to dust the work surface with confectioners' sugar and knead the sugar in until you get the right consistency.

3 Divide the mixture in 2. Add a tiny bit of pink food coloring to one half and knead it until the color is evenly mixed in. Add a tiny bit more coloring if you want a stronger color.

4 Break off walnut-sized pieces of mixture and roll into a cone shape. Pinch little ears on top of the narrow end. Squeeze the narrow end into a nose. Press a chocolate sprinkle into the face below the ears to make the eyes. Cut a length of twine about 2 inches and push it into the round end of the mouse to make the tail.

5 Use a toothpick to dab a tiny amount of pink food coloring on the nose. Put the mouse on the prepared baking sheet.

6 Repeat with the remaining mixture and let the mice dry out for at least 12 hours.

Advent numbered cookies

Vanilla shortbread

15 tablespoons unsalted butter, softened

2 cups all-purpose flour

½ teaspoon salt

½ cup confectioners' sugar, sifted

1 teaspoon vanilla extract

Chocolate shortbread

15 tablespoons butter, softened

1⅔ cups all-purpose flour

⅓ cup cocoa powder

½ teaspoon salt

½ cup confectioners' sugar, sifted

1 teaspoon vanilla extract

assorted cookie cutters, eg round, square, and oval

numbered cookie cutters

1–2 baking sheets, lined with baking parchment

24 cellophane bags

makes about 24

1 To make the vanilla shortbread, beat the butter in a mixing bowl with a wooden spoon until smooth and very soft. Meanwhile, sift together the flour and salt.

2 Add the confectioners' sugar to the creamed butter and continue mixing until light and fluffy. Add the vanilla and mix again. Add the sifted flour and salt and mix until it starts to come together into a dough.

3 To knead the dough, first sprinkle a little flour on a clean work surface. Then shape the dough into a ball and push on it and press it onto the work surface, turning it round often. Do this for a minute, then flatten into a disc, cover with plastic wrap, and chill until needed.

4 To make the chocolate shortbread, follow steps 1–3 above, but add the cocoa powder to the flour and salt.

5 Preheat the oven to 350°F.

6 Sprinkle more flour on the work surface. Using a rolling pin, roll out the vanilla and chocolate dough (separately) to a thickness of ⅛ inch and stamp out 24 shapes using the assorted cookie cutters. Arrange on the prepared baking sheets. Using the numbered cutters, stamp out numbers 1–24 and stick to each larger cookie with a dab of cold water.

7 Leave the cookies to chill in the fridge for 10 minutes.

8 Ask an adult to help you put one sheet on the middle shelf of the preheated oven. Bake for about 12 minutes, or until firm and starting to go crisp at the edges. Repeat with the second sheet of cookies.

9 Ask an adult to help you remove the cookies from the oven and let cool on the sheets before packaging into cellophane bags, if you like.

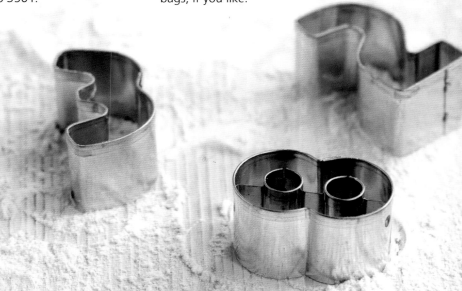

You will need a selection of numbered cookie cutters, preferably in different sizes, and plain cutters in different shapes to make these. Give them away to friends and family to celebrate Advent.

This is a very simple, edible Christmas decoration. Why not add some of your favorite candies to the garlands too?

68

popcorn garlands

safflower oil, for frying
popcorn kernels

*needle and assorted
    brightly colored threads*

1 Put 1 tablespoon of oil in a large saucepan. **Ask an adult to help you** put it over medium-high heat. Add enough popcorn to cover the base of the pan, cover tightly with a lid, and wait for the popping to start.

2 Holding the pan and lid firmly with oven mitts, give the pan a good shake from time to time.

3 When the popping stops, then all the kernels have popped and you can safely take off the lid and remove the pan from the heat. Tip the popcorn into a large bowl and let cool.

4 Thread the needle with a long piece of the colored thread and tie a big, double knot at the end. One by one, push a piece of popcorn onto the thread until you have a long garland. Repeat using different-colored threads.

5 Arrange the popcorn garlands on the Christmas tree or anywhere that you might need some edible decorations!

While you've got some popcorn on the go, why not make these perfect party nibbles?! They take just moments to make.

popcorn marshmallow clusters

1 tablespoon unsalted
    butter
2 cups mini-marshmallows
about 1½ cups popped
    popcorn
½ cup pecan pieces
½ cup dried cranberries
edible silver balls

*a baking sheet, lined with
    baking parchment*

makes loads!

1 Put the butter in a large saucepan. **Ask an adult to help you** put it over medium heat. Add the marshmallows and give them a good stir. Once they start to melt, add the popcorn, pecans, and cranberries. Stir constantly until the marshmallows melt and the mixture starts to clump together.

2 Carefully tip the mixture out of the pan and onto the prepared baking sheet. Scatter over some edible silver balls.

3 Once the mixture is cool enough to handle, break off clusters and serve in baskets or piled up on plates.

If you've ever been lucky enough to see a real shooting star, you'll no doubt have closed your eyes and made a wish. Ice these cute cookies in elaborate patterns and scatter with edible silver or gold balls so that they look as if they would shine brightly if they raced across the night sky.

gingerbread shooting stars

3 cups all-purpose flour

½ teaspoon baking powder

1 teaspoon baking soda

3 teaspoons ground ginger

½ teaspoon ground
cinnamon

a pinch of salt

1 stick unsalted butter,
softened

⅓ cup packed dark brown
sugar

1 egg, lightly beaten

⅓ cup corn syrup

Glacé Icing (page 8)

edible silver balls

*assorted shooting star-
shaped cookie cutters*

*2 baking sheets, lined with
baking parchment*

makes about 24

1 Sift together the flour, baking powder, baking soda, ginger, cinnamon, and salt in a mixing bowl.

2 Ask an adult to help you cream the butter and sugar together in the bowl of an electric mixer (or use a large bowl and an electric whisk). Add the beaten egg and corn syrup and mix until smooth. Add the sifted dry ingredients and mix again until smooth.

3 To knead the dough, first sprinkle a little flour on a clean work surface. Then shape the dough into a ball and push on it and press it onto the work surface, turning it round often. Do this for a minute, then flatten into a disc, cover with plastic wrap, and chill for a couple of hours until firm.

4 Preheat the oven to 350°F.

5 Sprinkle more flour on the work surface. Roll out the dough to a thickness of about ¼ inch. Stamp out shapes with the cookie cutters and arrange on the prepared baking sheets. Gather up any scraps of cookie dough, knead very lightly to bring together into a ball, and roll out again to stamp out more cookies. **Ask an adult to help you** put the sheets on the middle shelf of the preheated oven. Bake for about 10 minutes.

6 Ask an adult to help you remove the cookies from the oven and let cool on the sheets for a couple of minutes before transferring to a wire rack to cool completely.

7 Make a piping bag as described on page 16. Pipe Glacé Icing onto the cookies and decorate with silver balls. Leave on a wire rack to dry.

There's no cooking required for this edible, decorative idea, but it's an easy and fun way for small hands to get involved in the festive fun.

candy trees

assorted festive candies

roll of clear cellophane or cellophane bags

brightly colored ribbons

silver spray-painted branches and twigs

1 Tip all the candies into a large bowl and mix them up!

2 Ask an adult to help you cut large squares from the cellophane. You don't need to do this if you have cellophane bags already. Arrange a handful of candies in the middle of each square. Gather up the cellophane to make a pouch and tie with pretty festive ribbons, leaving enough ribbon to make a loop.

3 Arrange the silver branches and twigs in a sturdy vase. Hang the parcels on the tree.

I always used to make frosted fruit when I was little and it was piled high on a glass serving dish and given pride of place on the dinner table. Use a selection of green and red grapes, blueberries, and cranberries. In the summer months you could try frosting strands of jewel-like red currants.

frosted fruit

2 teaspoons dried
egg white or
meringue powder
1 bunch each
of green and
red grapes
a handful each
of cranberries

and blueberries
superfine sugar,
for sprinkling

*a baking sheet, lined
with baking
parchment*

makes a big plateful

1 In a large bowl, whisk the dried egg white and 2 tablespoons warm water with a balloon whisk until foamy. Using a pastry brush, brush the egg white over the fruit—try to cover them evenly and completely.

2 Hold the bunch of grapes above the prepared baking sheet and sprinkle superfine sugar over the grapes to cover completely.

3 Lightly brush the cranberries and blueberries with egg white and coat these in sugar too.

4 Let the fruit dry on the parchment for at least a couple of hours until the sugar has hardened and become crisp.

5 Arrange the fruit on a platter.

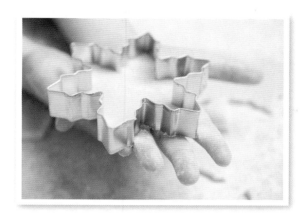

No two snowflakes are the same and these snowflake cookies are no exception. Look out for sets of fancy snowflake cookie cutters in all shapes and sizes and little pots of sparkly edible sprinkles to decorate your cookies with.

snowflake cookies

15 tablespoons unsalted butter, softened

1 cup sugar

1 egg, lightly beaten

½ teaspoon vanilla extract

a pinch of salt

3½ cups all-purpose flour

Glacé Icing (page 8)

edible white glitter

edible silver balls

assorted snowflake-shaped cookie cutters

2 baking sheets, lined with baking parchment

makes about 12, depending on size

1 Put the butter and sugar in the bowl of an electric mixer fitted with the paddle attachment (or use a large bowl and an electric whisk). **Ask an adult to help you** cream them until pale and fluffy. Add the beaten egg, vanilla, and salt and mix again.

2 Gradually add the flour and mix until incorporated and smooth. Tip the dough out onto the work surface, flatten into a disc, cover with plastic wrap, and chill for a couple of hours until firm.

3 Sprinkle a little flour on a clean work surface. Roll out the dough to a thickness of about ⅛ inch. Stamp out shapes with the cookie cutters and arrange on the prepared baking sheets. Gather up any scraps of cookie dough,

knead very lightly to bring together into a ball, and roll out again to stamp out more cookies. Chill in the fridge for a further 15 minutes.

4 Preheat the oven to 350°F.

5 Ask an adult to help you put the baking sheets on the middle shelf of the preheated oven. Bake for about 10–12 minutes until pale golden and firm to the touch.

6 Ask an adult to help you remove the sheets from the oven. Let the cookies cool on the baking sheets before transferring to a wire rack to cool completely.

7 Make a piping bag as described on page 16. Pipe Glacé Icing onto the cookies and dust with glitter. Decorate with silver balls.

cakes & desserts

This is a chocolate cake baked in a jelly roll pan, and then rolled up and decorated to look like a wooden log. This is traditionally what French people eat for dessert on Christmas Eve. Try it and see if you like it!

bûche de Noël

1 cup self-rising flour
3 tablespoons cocoa
    powder
4 eggs
¾ cup sugar
Chocolate Frosting
    (page 9)
confectioners' sugar,
    for dusting

Chocolate bark
5 oz. chocolate (milk or
    bittersweet)

*a 14 x 10-in. jelly roll pan,
    greased and lined with
    greased baking
    parchment*

*a large sheet of baking
    parchment, sprinkled
    with superfine sugar*

*2 robins, to decorate
    (optional)*

serves 8

1 Preheat the oven to 375°F.

2 Dust the prepared jelly roll pan with a little flour. Tip out the excess flour.

3 Sift the self-rising flour and cocoa together onto a piece of baking parchment.

4 Break the eggs in the bowl of an electric mixer (or use a large bowl and an electric whisk). Add the sugar and **ask an adult to help you** mix on medium-high speed for about 5 minutes until the mixture is very light, pale, and foamy, and has doubled in size.

5 Gently tip the flour and cocoa mixture into the bowl and fold in using a large metal spoon. Carefully tip the mixture into the prepared pan and spread it right to the edges, being careful not to knock out too much air.

6 Ask an adult to help you put the pan on the middle shelf of the preheated oven. Bake for 9–10 minutes until the cake bounces back when lightly pressed with your finger. Be careful not to burn your finger!

7 Ask an adult to help you remove the pan from the oven. Using oven mitts, tip the warm cake out of the pan and upside down onto the prepared sheet of baking parchment. With one

of the long sides nearest you, carefully peel off the parchment. Roll up the cake with the sugar-dusted paper rolled inside the cake. Set aside to cool.

8 Make up the Chocolate Frosting as described on page 9. You may need to leave it somewhere cool for 30 minutes to thicken enough to spread.

9 Unroll the cake and spread the surface with one-third of the frosting. Carefully roll the log back up completely, without the paper this time. Slice one-third off the end at an angle. Arrange the larger piece on a serving plate with the join underneath. Position the smaller third at an angle on one side. Spread the remaining frosting over the cake to cover it.

10 To make the bark, **ask an adult to help you** put the chocolate in a heatproof bowl over a pan of simmering water or in the microwave on a low setting. Stir very carefully until melted.

11 Spread the melted chocolate in a thin layer on a sheet of baking parchment. Let set, then break into pieces. Stick the bark onto the log and dust with confectioners' sugar. Decorate with robins, if you like.

This is a delicious French gingerbread cake. Make it a couple of days before you want to eat it so that the flavors of all the spices mixed with the honey will taste much better. Serve it in slices on its own or with a lick of butter.

pain d'épices

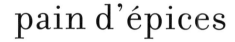

1¾ cups all-purpose flour

2 teaspoons baking powder

1 teaspoon ground cinnamon

3 teaspoons ground ginger

¼ teaspoon each ground cloves, allspice, and salt

10 tablespoons unsalted butter, softened

⅓ cup packed light brown sugar

½ cup honey

2 eggs, lightly beaten

3–4 tablespoons milk

a 2-lb. loaf pan, greased

makes 10 slices

1 Preheat the oven to 350°F and baseline the prepared loaf pan with greased baking parchment.

2 Sift the flour, baking powder, and spices together into a mixing bowl and set aside.

3 Put the butter and sugar in the bowl of an electric mixer (or use a large bowl and an electric whisk). **Ask an adult to help you** cream them until pale and light.

4 Add the honey and mix again. Gradually add the beaten eggs, mixing well between each addition and scraping down the bowl with a rubber spatula from time to time.

5 Add the sifted dry ingredients and the milk and mix again until smooth. Spoon into the prepared pan and spread evenly with a knife.

6 **Ask an adult to help you** put the pan on the middle shelf of the preheated oven. Bake for about 1 hour, or until well risen and a skewer inserted into the middle of the cake comes out clean. You may need to cover the cake loosely with a sheet of foil if it is browning too quickly.

7 **Ask an adult to help you** remove the cake from the oven. Let it cool in the pan for 5 minutes before tipping out onto a wire rack to cool completely.

Nothing says Christmas like a gingerbread house and this one is straight out of a fairy tale. You could decorate the cake with any number and type of candies, so let your imagination run wild. Be aware that you will need to make up the recipe twice.

gingerbread house

Make up this recipe twice

3 cups all-purpose flour

½ teaspoon baking powder

1 teaspoon baking soda

3 teaspoons ground ginger

½ teaspoon ground cinnamon

¼ teaspoon each of ground cloves and allspice

a pinch of salt

1 stick unsalted butter, softened

⅓ cup dark brown sugar

1 egg, lightly beaten

⅓ cup corn syrup

2–3 cups royal icing sugar

assorted candies

3 baking sheets, lined with baking parchment

a piping bag, fitted with a plain tip

serves 12

1 Sift the flour, baking powder, baking soda, and spices together into a mixing bowl and set aside.

2 Put the butter and brown sugar in the bowl of an electric mixer (or use a large bowl and an electric whisk). **Ask an adult to help you** cream them until fluffy.

3 Add the beaten egg and corn syrup and mix until smooth. Add the sifted dry ingredients and mix again until smooth.

4 Sprinkle a little flour on a clean work surface. Shape the dough into a ball and push on it and press it onto the work surface, turning it round often. Do this for a minute, then flatten into a disc, cover with plastic wrap, and chill for a couple of hours until firm.

5 Repeat steps 1–4 to make a second quantity of gingerbread dough.

6 When you are ready to bake the house, preheat the oven to 350°F.

7 You will need to make paper templates for the walls and roof of your house. Take a large sheet of paper and draw a rectangle measuring 8 x 4½ inches for the roof. Make another paper rectangle measuring 7½ x 4 inches for the front and back walls. You will also need a template for the sides —this will be a 4-inch square with a 1½-inch high triangle on top.

8 Sprinkle more flour on the work surface. Using a rolling pin, roll out the dough to a thickness of about ⅛ inch. Use your paper templates to cut out 2 roof shapes, 2 big walls, and 2 sides. You may find it easier to write on the baking parchment which shapes are which as you cut them out. Arrange them on the prepared baking sheets. Carefully cut out windows from the walls and sides.

9 Gather up any scraps of dough, knead very lightly to bring together into a ball, and roll out again to stamp out any other cookie shapes that you like. Why not make the carrots for Santa and Rudolf's tray (see page 56)?

10 **Ask an adult to help you** put the sheets on the middle shelf of the preheated oven.

You will need to bake the gingerbread in batches. Bake for about 10–15 minutes until firm and just starting to brown at the edges.

11 Ask an adult to help you remove the gingerbread from the oven and let cool completely.

12 Use the royal icing sugar to make icing according to the manufacturer's instructions. It will need to be thick enough to hold its shape when piped, so add the water gradually until you have the correct consistency. Fill the piping bag with the icing. You will need 2 pairs of hands for the next step!

13 Take one gingerbread side and pipe a line of icing along the bottom and up one side (just up to but not including the gables). Hold it up on a serving tray or platter. Take a big wall and pipe some icing along the bottom and 2 sides. Hold this at

a right angle to the first, iced side. Pick up the second big wall and pipe some icing along the bottom and 2 sides. Hold this in place opposite the other wall and so that it meets the side at a right angle. Repeat with the remaining side. You may find it easier to position cans or jars inside the house to hold the walls in place until the icing has set firm.

14 Once the walls are set and secure, you can attach the roof. Pipe a line of icing down the gables and position one roof panel on either side of the gables. Pipe a line of icing across the top of the roof. Hold the roof in place until the icing feels firm.

15 To decorate the house, pipe royal-icing patterns onto the roof panels and decorate with your choice of candies. Pipe borders around the windows and doors, as well as along the bottom of the house, and decorate with candies as you like.

mini baked Alaskas

4 x ½-in. thick slices of
storebought chocolate
loaf cake
2 tablespoons jam or
chocolate spread
4 scoops of premium
vanilla ice cream
2 egg whites
⅔ cup superfine sugar

a 2¼-inch round cookie
cutter

a baking sheet, lined with
baking parchment

makes 4

1 Preheat the oven to 475°F.

2 Using the cookie cutter, stamp out a round from each slice of chocolate cake and place on the prepared baking sheet. Spread ½ tablespoon jam over each round, top with a scoop of ice cream, and freeze.

3 Place the egg whites in a large, clean mixing bowl with the salt. **Ask an adult to help you** use an electric whisk to beat the egg whites until they're nice and thick. When you turn the whisk off and lift them up slowly, the egg whites should stand in stiff peaks.

4 Gradually add the sugar, beating well after each addition, then whisk for a further minute until the meringue is very stiff and glossy.

5 Using a palette knife, cover each ball of ice cream and cake with meringue. **Ask an adult to help you** put the sheet on the middle shelf of the preheated oven. Bake for 2–3 minutes, or until the meringue begins to turn golden at the edges. Serve immediately.

Who doesn't like ice cream and meringue? Put the two together and you've got the perfect dessert. You could use whichever flavor of ice cream you like. You could assemble the Alaskas in advance and keep them in the freezer for a couple of hours. Simply bake in the oven when you're ready.

Look for sparkling pomegranate or cranberry drinks to make these fun gelatin desserts. Whisking the mixture just before it sets traps the bubbles to give the desserts a pretty frosted look.

fruity treats

8 leaves of gelatin

3 cups either sparkling grape, raspberry, or cranberry juice, or pomegranate lemonade

3–4 tablespoons superfine sugar, or to taste

1 pomegranate, seeds scooped out

3½ oz. seedless red grapes, halved

1 cup blueberries

serves 6–8

1 Soak the gelatin leaves in a bowl of cold water for 5 minutes.

2 Put 1 cup of the juice and the sugar in a saucepan. **Ask an adult to help you** put it over medium heat and heat until just below boiling point.

3 Drain the gelatin leaves, add to the hot juice and stir well until the gelatin is thoroughly dissolved.

4 Pour the remaining juice into a large bowl, add the hot juice and gelatin mixture, and mix well with a whisk to combine. Chill in the fridge until starting to set.

5 Meanwhile, set aside about 5 tablespoons of the pomegranate seeds. Mix together the remaining pomegranate seeds, the grapes, and blueberries.

6 Once the mixture has started to set, you need to make it bubbly. Quickly whisk with a balloon whisk to make air bubbles. Fold in the fruit and divide between 6–8 small glasses.

7 Cover with plastic wrap and chill in the fridge until completely set.

8 Top each serving with the reserved pomegranate seeds, to decorate.

Cover this cake with mountains of snowy frosting and a scattering of coconut chips. You'll need a candy thermometer to make the frosting, and once it is made, you have to work quickly, as it sets fast!

coconut cake

13 tablespoons unsalted butter, softened

1 cup sugar

4 eggs, lightly beaten

1 teaspoon vanilla extract

1¼ cups all-purpose flour

4 teaspoons baking powder

a pinch of salt

½ cup desiccated coconut

3 tablespoons sour cream or coconut cream, at room temperature

2 cups dried coconut chips

Seven-minute frosting

¾ cup sugar

3 egg whites

2 x 8-in. round cake pans, greased and baselined with greased baking parchment

a candy thermometer

serves 8–10

1 Preheat the oven to 350°F.

2 Put the butter and sugar in the bowl of an electric mixer (or use a large bowl and an electric whisk). **Ask an adult to help you** cream them until pale and light.

3 Gradually add the beaten eggs, mixing well between each addition and scraping down the side of the bowl with a rubber spatula from time to time. Add the vanilla and mix.

4 Sift the flour, baking powder, and salt into the bowl and add the desiccated coconut. Fold the dry ingredients into the cake mixture until just mixed using a large metal spoon or rubber spatula. Add the sour cream and mix again until smooth.

5 Divide the mixture between the prepared cake pans. **Ask an adult to help you** put the pans on the middle shelf of the preheated oven. Bake for 20–25 minutes until golden and a skewer inserted into the middle of the cakes comes out clean.

6 **Ask an adult to help you** remove the pans from the oven. Let cool for 5 minutes before tipping the cakes out onto a wire rack.

7 To make the Seven-Minute Frosting, **ask an adult to help you**. Put the sugar, egg whites, and 2 teaspoons water into a large heatproof bowl. Set the bowl over a pan of simmering water—the bottom of the bowl should not touch the water. Whisk slowly with a balloon whisk to dissolve the sugar. Continue cooking and whisking until the mixture reaches 140°F on a candy thermometer. The meringue should double in volume and be hot to touch.

8 Transfer the mixture to a free-standing electric mixer fitted with the whisk attachment (or keep it in the same bowl and use an electric whisk). Continue to whisk on medium speed until the meringue is stiff and very glossy. The frosting is now ready to use straightaway.

9 Place one cake on a serving plate and spread 3–4 heaping tablespoons of the frosting on top. Top with the second cake layer. Working quickly with a palette knife, cover the top and sides of the cake with the frosting, fluffing the frosting into peaks as you do so.

10 Scatter the coconut chips all over the cake and set to one side to allow the frosting to dry for about 30 minutes before serving.

This classic recipe can be whipped up in no time using a storebought pie crust and a can of pumpkin purée.

pumpkin pie

single pie crust dough

1–2 tablespoons milk

14-oz. can puréed pumpkin

2 eggs

1 egg yolk

**¾ cup packed light
    brown sugar**

**1 teaspoon ground
    cinnamon**

½ teaspoon ground ginger

**a pinch each of grated
    nutmeg, ground cloves,
    and salt**

½ cup heavy cream

**2–3 teaspoons granulated
    sugar**

**confectioners' sugar,
    for dusting**

a 9-in. pie plate

a small star-shaped cutter

serves 6

1 Preheat the oven to 350°F and place a baking sheet on the middle shelf to preheat.

2 Sprinkle a little flour on a clean work surface. Roll the pie dough until it's big enough to fit your pie plate. Carefully lift up the pastry (it may help to lift it while on the rolling pin) and lay it in the pie plate. Carefully trim any excess pastry from around the edge with a small knife.

3 Gather up any scraps of dough, knead very lightly to bring together into a ball, and roll out again. Use the star-shaped cutter to stamp out lots of stars. Brush the edges of the pie with a little milk and stick the pastry stars, slightly overlapping, all around the edge.

4 Chill the pie crust in the fridge while you prepare the filling.

5 Put the pumpkin, whole eggs and yolk, brown sugar, spices, and cream in a large bowl and whisk until well mixed and smooth.

6 Carefully pour the mixture into the pie crust, brush the stars with a little more milk, and scatter the granulated sugar over them.

7 Ask an adult to help you put the pie on the hot baking sheet in the preheated oven. Bake for about 35 minutes, or until the filling has set and the pastry is golden brown.

8 Ask an adult to help you remove the pie from the oven. Let cool to room temperature before dusting with confectioners' sugar.

This is a simple fruitcake that can be decorated any number of ways, but with its crown of sparkling, jewelled dried fruits, it makes a beautiful teatime treat.

easy fruitcake

½ cup glacé cherries, chopped, plus extra, whole, to decorate

¼ cup candied mixed peel

1 lb. mixed dried fruit (eg raisins, currants, chopped dried apricots)

1¾ cups all-purpose flour

1 teaspoon baking powder

1 teaspoon apple pie spice

a pinch of salt

1½ sticks unsalted butter, softened

¾ cup sugar

3 eggs, lightly beaten

¼ cup ground almonds

2–3 tablespoons milk

apricot jam, chopped dried apricots, blanched almonds, pecan halves, to decorate

a deep, 8-in. round cake pan

serves 8–10

1 Preheat the oven to 325°F. **Ask an adult to help you** line the base and side of the cake pan with a double thickness of baking parchment.

2 Mix the chopped glacé cherries, mixed peel, and dried fruit together in a bowl.

3 Sift the flour, baking powder, apple pie spice, and salt together in another bowl.

4 Put the butter and sugar in the bowl of an electric mixer (or use a large bowl and an electric whisk). **Ask an adult to help you** cream them until pale and light.

5 Gradually add the beaten eggs, mixing well between each addition and scraping down the sides of the bowl with a rubber spatula from time to time.

6 Add the dried fruit and stir to mix.

7 Add the sifted dry ingredients and the ground almonds to the mixture and fold in using a large metal spoon or rubber spatula.

8 Add the milk and mix until smooth.

9 Spoon the mixture into the prepared cake pan and spread evenly.

10 **Ask an adult to help you** put the pan on the middle shelf of the preheated oven. Bake for 30 minutes, then turn the heat down to 300°F. Continue to bake for a further 1½ hours, or until a skewer inserted into the middle of the cake comes out clean.

11 **Ask an adult to help you** remove the cake from the oven and let cool in the pan.

12 Once the cake is completely cold, tip it out of the pan and carefully peel off the paper.

13 **Ask an adult to help you** put about 5 tablespoons apricot jam in a small saucepan over low heat. Leave until runny, then strain.

14 Brush the top of the cake with a thin layer of the jam. Arrange the glacé cherries, apricots, and nuts in a pattern on top. Brush with a little more jam to glaze, then let set.

*This is the perfect cake for a Christmas party,
as it will feed a good crowd of hungry mouths.*

Frosty the snowman

Medium Cake (page 8)

Large Cake (page 8)

Buttercream Frosting
  (page 9)

red food coloring paste

4 cups desiccated coconut

1 large storebought
  cupcake

1 short licorice twizzler

chocolate chips

4 red sugar-coated candies

1½ oz. white ready-to-use
  fondant or royal icing

orange food coloring
  paste

2 short lengths of flaked
  chocolate

*a 7-in. round cake pan,
  greased and baselined
  with greased baking
  parchment*

*a 9-in. round cake pan,
  greased and baselined
  with greased baking
  parchment*

a length of ribbon

serves at least 14

1 Preheat the oven to 350°F.

2 Make up the Medium Cake and Large Cake as described on page 8. Spoon the medium cake batter into the prepared 7-inch cake pan and the large cake batter into the 9-inch cake pan. Spread evenly.

3 Ask an adult to help you put the pans on the middle shelf of the preheated oven. Bake the medium cake for about 30 minutes and the large cake for 35–40 minutes, or until a skewer inserted into the middle of the cakes comes out clean.

4 Ask an adult to help you remove the pans from the oven and let cool for 10 minutes before tipping the cakes out to cool on a wire rack.

5 While the cakes are cooling, take the Buttercream Frosting and put 5 tablespoons into a small bowl. Tint this small amount red using the food coloring paste.

6 Lay the cold cakes side by side. If necessary, cut a thin layer off the tops of the cakes so that they are the same height. Cut away about one-fifth off the larger cake in an inward curve and set aside. Lay the ribbon down horizontally before fitting the smaller cake on the ribbon into the curved space.

7 Cover the top and side of both of the cakes in the untinted buttercream, spreading it evenly with a palette knife. Cover the whole cake evenly in desiccated coconut.

8 Use the reserved leaf-shaped piece of cake and the cupcake to make the snowman's hat. Cover these in the red buttercream and position on top of the snowman's head.

9 Cut the licorice in half for the eyes and arrange the chocolate chips for the mouth. Position the sugar-coated candies down the center as buttons.

10 Tint the fondant icing orange using the food coloring paste and shape this into a carrot. Position on the snowman's face.

11 Finally, push a length of flaked chocolate into each side for the snowman's arms.

marble cake

1 Preheat the oven to 350°F. Line the base and ends of each loaf pan with a strip of greased baking parchment.

2 Ask an adult to help you put the chocolate in a heatproof bowl over a pan of barely simmering water or in the microwave on a low setting. Stir very carefully until melted.

3 Sift the flour and baking powder together into a bowl.

4 Put the butter and sugar in the bowl of an electric mixer (or use a large bowl and an electric whisk). **Ask an adult to help you** cream them until pale and light.

5 Gradually add the beaten eggs, mixing well between each addition and scraping down the side of the bowl with a rubber spatula from time to time. Add the vanilla and mix.

6 Tip the sifted flour and baking powder into the batter and mix until smooth. Stir in the milk. Spoon one-third of this mixture into the melted chocolate. Mix until smooth.

7 Using a tablespoon, drop alternate spoonfuls of vanilla and chocolate batter into one of the prepared loaf pans. When it's half full, give the pan a sharp tap on the work surface to level the mixture. To create a marbled effect, drag the blade of a table knife through the mixture to create swirls. Do not over-swirl the mixture or the effect will not be so dramatic. Repeat this step with the second loaf pan.

8 Ask an adult to help you put the pans on the middle shelf of the preheated oven. Bake for about 40 minutes or until a skewer inserted into the middle of the cakes comes out clean.

9 Ask an adult to help you remove the pans from the oven. Let cool for 15 minutes before carefully lifting the cakes out of the pans and onto a wire rack to cool completely.

10 Spread the Chocolate Frosting over the tops of each cold cake and decorate with assorted chocolate sprinkles. You will have some frosting left over—why not use it to frost the Frosted Brownie Squares on page 12?

2 oz. bittersweet
   chocolate, chopped
1⅓ cups all-purpose flour
1 heaping teaspoon
   baking powder
1½ sticks unsalted butter,
   softened
1 cup sugar
4 eggs, lightly beaten
1 teaspoon vanilla extract
2 tablespoons milk
Chocolate Frosting
   (page 9)
chocolate sprinkles

2 x 1-lb. loaf pans, greased

serves 8–10

This cake keeps really well in an airtight box and can be made a day in advance. Don't be tempted to over-swirl the mixtures or the marble effect will be less dramatic. This recipe makes two smaller cakes—one to eat and one to give away—but can just as easily be made in one 2-lb. loaf pan.

party food

Christmas drinks

hot chocolate

**1½ oz. semisweet
chocolate drops
1⅓ cups whole milk
a few drops vanilla extract
2 teaspoons sugar or
honey, or to taste
1 tablespoon whipped
heavy cream or squirty
cream from a can
mini-marshmallows**

serves 1

1 Tip the chocolate drops into a heatproof glass or mug.

2 Put the milk, vanilla, and sugar in a small saucepan. **Ask an adult to help you** set it over medium heat and heat until just boiling, then whisk with a balloon whisk until foamy.

3 Pour the hot milk over the chocolate drops and stir until the chocolate has melted. Taste and add a little more sugar if needed.

4 Dollop the cream on the top, scatter with mini-marshmallows, and serve immediately.

mulled apple juice

**4 cups pure apple juice
1 cinnamon stick
4 whole cloves
2 tablespoons honey
1 orange
2–3 small Macoun apples**

makes about 4 cups

1 Pour the apple juice into a saucepan and add the cinnamon stick, whole cloves, and honey.

2 Remove the peel from the orange in strips using a vegetable peeler and add to the pan.

3 Cut the apples into quarters and remove the cores. Thinly slice the apples and tip them into the apple juice. **Ask an adult to help you** put the pan over medium heat and bring the juice to a gentle simmer. Cook for 5 minutes.

4 Ladle the mulled apple juice into cups or mugs and serve.

These are perfect
drinks to warm you
up when it's chilly
outside. The hot
chocolate is made
with real chocolate
and a few drops of
vanilla extract to
make it that little bit
more special. The
mulled apple juice is
your opportunity to
join in with the adults
when they indulge in
their own spiced
mulled wine!

No party is complete without a heaped dish of hot bite-sized pigs in blankets. All you need to add is a bowl of ketchup to serve with them.

pigs in blankets

12 oz. puff pastry dough, thawed if frozen
1 tablespoon Dijon mustard
24 cocktail sausages
1 egg, lightly beaten

a baking sheet, lined with baking parchment

makes 24

1 Preheat the oven to 375°F.

2 Sprinkle a little flour on a clean work surface. Unroll the pastry, and if it's thicker than 1/16 inch, use a rolling pin to make it the right thickness. Spread the mustard over the pastry.

3 With the long side of the pastry nearest you, cut the pastry vertically into 6 equal strips. Cut each strip into 4. Place a sausage on each piece of pastry and roll the pastry around it. Arrange on the prepared baking sheet.

4 Score 2 or 3 small cuts in the top of each roll with a sharp knife and brush with the beaten egg.

5 Ask an adult to help you put the sheet on the middle shelf of the preheated oven. Bake for 30 minutes, or until golden.

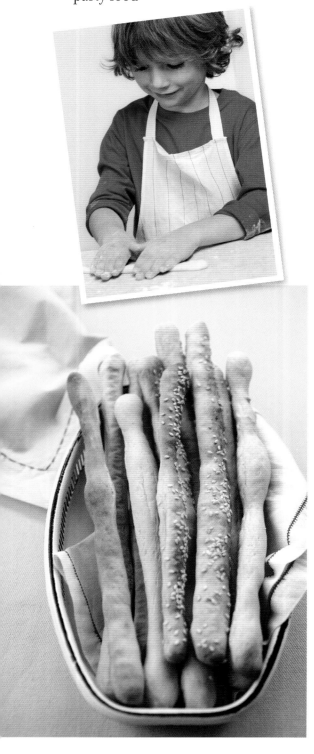

These Italian-style grissini sticks have Parmesan added to the dough to make them a little more interesting. Grissini are delicious eaten on their own or served with dips or soup.

cheesy grissini

3 cups bread flour

1 package (¼ oz.) dry yeast

1 teaspoon fine sea salt

¾ cup warm water

1 tablespoon olive oil

3 tablespoons finely grated Parmesan

1–2 tablespoons sesame seeds (optional)

2 or more baking sheets, lined with baking parchment

makes about 24

1 Sift the flour into a large mixing bowl and stir in the yeast and salt. Make a hole like a well in the middle and pour in three-quarters of the water and all the oil. Stir with a wooden spoon—the dough should be soft but not too sticky.

2 Add the grated Parmesan to the dough. It will get mixed in when you knead the dough.

3 To knead the dough, sprinkle a little flour on a clean work surface. Shape the dough into a ball and push on it and press it onto the work surface, turning it round often. You'll need to keep doing this until it is silky smooth and elastic—about 7 minutes.

4 Shape the dough into a neat ball again. Wash and dry the mixing bowl and sit the dough back in it. Cover tightly with plastic wrap and leave in a warm place until the dough has doubled in size—at least 1 hour.

5 Preheat the oven to 400°F.

6 Tip the dough onto the floured work surface and knead for 1 minute. Divide it into walnut-sized pieces and roll each piece into a long stick using your hands. Arrange on the prepared baking sheets and let rise again for a further 10 minutes.

7 Brush some of the grissini with water and sprinkle the sesame seeds over them, if using.

8 Ask an adult to help you put one of the sheets on the middle shelf of the preheated oven. Bake for 7–8 minutes, or until crisp and golden brown.

9 Repeat with the remaining grissini.

This recipe makes a large pot of soup—enough to feed a hungry crowd on a cold winter's day. If you don't like things too spicy, leave out the red chile.

butternut squash soup with cheesy croutons

1 onion, peeled

1 medium leek

1 celery rib

2 carrots, peeled

2 tablespoons unsalted
butter

1 tablespoon olive oil

1½ lbs. peeled butternut
squash chunks

1 garlic clove, crushed

1 red chile, seeded and
finely chopped

1 in. fresh ginger, peeled
and grated

4 cups vegetable stock

sea salt and freshly ground
black pepper

Croutons

6 slices of 1-day-old bread
(preferably sourdough)

1 tablespoon olive oil

2 cups grated cheddar or
Parmesan

makes a large pot!

1 Ask an adult to help you chop the onion, leek, celery, and carrots into small pieces.

2 Put the butter and oil in a large saucepan. Ask an adult to help you set it over medium heat. Add the chopped onion, leek, celery, and carrots and cook slowly until they are soft but not browned.

3 Add the squash, garlic, chile, and ginger to the pan and continue to cook for a further 3–4 minutes.

4 Add the stock and season with salt and pepper. Bring to a boil, then lower the heat so that the soup is at a gentle simmer and continue to cook until the squash is tender.

5 Ask an adult to help you blend the soup until smooth either in a blender or using a stick blender. Check the seasoning and add more salt or pepper if needed. If the soup is a little thick, add some extra stock.

6 To make the croutons, preheat the oven to 350°F.

7 Cut the bread into chunks and tip into a large bowl. Add the oil and mix with your hands so that the chunks are coated in oil. Add the grated cheese and stir well. Tip the croutons out onto a baking sheet.

8 Ask an adult to help you put the sheet in the preheated oven. Bake for 15 minutes, or until golden and crisp.

9 Ladle the soup into bowls and scatter some croutons on top. Any leftover soup can be left to cool and then frozen in an airtight box.

French toast is such a nice thing to have as a treat for breakfast. Why not surprise your family and make a batch for everyone early on Christmas morning? You will need just a little help from an adult.

French toast

4 eggs

¼ cup milk

a good pinch of ground cinnamon

1 teaspoon vanilla extract

1 tablespoon pure maple syrup, plus extra for drizzling

12 slices of brioche, white bread, or panettone

4 tablespoons unsalted butter

confectioners' sugar, for dusting

a star-shaped cookie cutter

serves 4

1 Put the eggs, milk, cinnamon, vanilla, and maple syrup in a mixing bowl and whisk with a balloon whisk.

2 Lay the bread slices out on a cutting board and, using the star-shaped cutter, stamp out a star from the middle of each slice.

3 Ask an adult to help you melt half the butter in a large skillet over medium-high heat.

4 Dip half the bread stars into the egg mixture and allow to soak thoroughly on both sides.

5 Add the eggy stars to the hot skillet—you will need to fry them in batches because you should have just one layer of stars in the skillet at a time. Cook for about 1 minute or until they turn golden.

6 Turn the stars over and cook the other sides for another minute.

7 Repeat with the remaining butter and stars. You will have 3 per person. Dust with confectioners' sugar and drizzle with maple syrup to serve.

buttermilk pancakes

1¾ cups all-purpose flour

3 teaspoons baking
  powder

½ teaspoon salt

¼ cup sugar

3 tablespoons unsalted
  butter, plus extra
  for frying

½ cup milk

½ cup buttermilk

2 eggs, lightly beaten

1 teaspoon vanilla extract

pure maple syrup, to serve

crispy cooked bacon slices,
  to serve (optional)

makes 16–18

1 Sift the flour, baking powder, salt, and sugar into a large mixing bowl and make a hole like a well in the middle.

2 Ask an adult to help you melt the butter in a small saucepan over low heat or in the microwave on a low setting.

3 Put the milk, buttermilk, eggs, melted butter, and vanilla in small bowl and whisk with a balloon whisk. Pour into the dry ingredients and whisk until the batter is smooth.

4 Put a pat of butter in a large, heavy skillet. **Ask an adult to help you** set it over medium heat. Allow the butter to melt, swirling it so that it coats the bottom of the skillet evenly.

5 Drop a ladleful of the pancake batter into the hot skillet and cook for about 1 minute, or until bubbles start to appear on the surface. Using a spatula, flip the pancake over and cook the other side until the pancake is golden and well risen. Remove the pancake from the skillet and keep it warm on a plate covered with foil.

6 Repeat with the remaining batter.

7 Serve the pancakes with crisp bacon, if you like, and a drizzle of maple syrup.

What better way to start Christmas morning than with a mile-high stack of these pancakes? Serve with a good glug of maple syrup and crisp bacon slices.

cheese & ham scones

1¾ cups all-purpose flour

**2 teaspoons baking
  powder**

a pinch of salt

**½ teaspoon mustard
  powder (optional)**

**3 tablespoons unsalted
  butter, chilled and diced**

**½ cup grated cheddar,
  plus extra for sprinkling**

½ cup diced ham

1 egg, lightly beaten

⅓–½ cup milk

a 2-in. round cookie cutter

*a baking sheet, lined with
  baking parchment*

makes 8–10

1 Preheat the oven to 400°F.

2 Sift the flour, baking powder, salt, and mustard powder, if using, into a large mixing bowl. Add the chilled, diced butter and rub in using your fingertips.

3 Add three-quarters of the cheese and all the ham and mix well. Make a hole like a well in the middle. Pour in the beaten egg and enough milk to make a soft dough.

4 Sprinkle a little flour on a clean work surface. Use a rolling pin to roll out the dough until it is about ¾ inch thick. Stamp out rounds with the cookie cutter and arrange the scones on the prepared baking sheet.

5 Brush the scones with a little milk and scatter a little more cheese over the tops. **Ask an adult to help you** put the sheet on the middle shelf of the preheated oven. Bake for about 10–12 minutes until golden brown.

6 Ask an adult to help you remove the sheet from the oven and tip the scones onto a wire rack to cool.

Scones are so delicious
and so easy to make.
Serve these little
cheesy nuggets still
warm from the oven
or with a bowl of
steaming soup.

You could easily serve these as a fancy appetizer on Christmas day. The pancakes can be made in advance and frozen—simply wrap them in foil and warm in the oven before serving.

Scotch pancakes with smoked salmon

1 cup all-purpose flour

1 teaspoon baking powder

a large pinch of salt

1 egg

⅔–¾ cup milk

1–2 tablespoons safflower
    oil

To serve

6½ oz. smoked salmon

10 teaspoons crème
    fraîche or sour cream

1 tablespoon finely
    snipped chives

makes about 20

1 Sift the flour, baking powder, and salt into a large mixing bowl. Break the egg into the bowl and gradually pour in the milk, mixing all the time with a balloon whisk. You may not need to add all the milk—the batter should be smooth and thick.

2 Ask an adult to help you preheat a griddle pan or heavy skillet over medium heat. Pour a little of the oil in the pan and swirl it to coat the base of the pan evenly. Let it heat up.

3 Drop a tablespoon of batter into the hot pan for each pancake—you will probably only be able to cook 4 pancakes at a time. Cook for about 1 minute, or until bubbles start to appear on the surface and the underside is golden. Using a spatula, flip the pancakes over and cook the other side until the pancakes are golden.

4 Remove the pancakes from the pan and keep them warm on a plate covered with foil.

5 Repeat with the remaining batter.

6 To serve, snip the smoked salmon into pieces. Dollop ½ teaspoon crème fraîche onto each pancake and top with the salmon. Finish with a sprinkle of snipped chives.

bagel chips

4 plain bagels
3–4 tablespoons olive oil
sea salt flakes
2 teaspoons dried oregano
1 teaspoon Spanish
smoked paprika
2 tablespoons grated
Parmesan

makes about 32

1 Preheat the oven to 350°F.

2 Cut each bagel in half to make semi-circles. Put one half cut-side down and carefully slice the bagel vertically, as thinly as possible. Repeat with the remaining bagels and lay the slices on baking sheets in a single layer. Brush each slice with olive oil. Sprinkle a quarter of the slices with salt, a quarter with oregano, a quarter with paprika, and a quarter with cheese.

3 Ask an adult to help you bake them in the preheated oven for 15 minutes, or until golden and crisp.

savory dips

Dips are perfect for parties—serve them with Bagel Chips (page 118) or Cheesy Grissini (page 107).

red pepper & chickpea dip

2 red bell peppers
2 tablespoons olive oil
14-oz. can of chickpeas
juice of ½ lemon
1 heaping tablespoon Greek yogurt

1 small garlic clove, crushed (optional)
a pinch of cayenne pepper (optional)
sea salt and freshly ground black pepper

makes a bowlful

1 Preheat the broiler.

2 Cut the bell peppers in half and scoop out the seeds with a spoon. Arrange the peppers on the broiler pan, skin-side up. Drizzle with the olive oil and **ask an adult to help you** put them under the hot broiler. Broil until the skins of the peppers are blackened and charred. Tip the hot peppers into a bowl, cover with plastic wrap, and let cool for about 10 minutes.

3 When the peppers are cool, peel off the skins and throw them away. Put the peppers in the bowl of a food processor. Drain the chickpeas in a strainer and rinse under cold water. Add to the peppers. Add the lemon juice, yogurt, garlic, and cayenne, if using, and season with salt and pepper.

4 **Ask an adult to help you** whizz the ingredients until they are almost smooth. Taste and add more lemon, salt, or pepper if needed.

avocado dip

2 ripe avocados
1 ripe tomato
juice of 1 lemon
a dash of Worcestershire sauce

sea salt and freshly ground black pepper

makes a bowlful

1 **Ask an adult to help you** cut the avocados in half and remove the pits. Use a spoon to scoop out the flesh from each half and place in a mixing bowl. Mash the avocado with a fork until it is almost smooth.

2 Chop the tomato into small pieces and add to the avocado with the lemon juice and Worcestershire sauce. Mix well, then season with salt and pepper.

cream cheese & herb dip

1¼ cups cream cheese
3 tablespoons Greek yogurt
juice of ½ lemon
1 tablespoon finely chopped parsley
1 tablespoons finely snipped chives

1 small garlic clove, crushed (optional)
sea salt and freshly ground black pepper

makes a bowlful

1 Put the cream cheese in a mixing bowl and beat with a wooden spoon until slightly softened. Stir in the yogurt, lemon juice, herbs, and garlic, if using. Season to taste with salt and pepper.

Palmiers can be savory or sweet. These ones are filled with pesto and grated Parmesan, but you could also try scattering the rolled-out pastry with sugar and cinnamon.

pesto palmiers

12 oz. puff pastry dough, thawed if frozen
2 tablespoons red pesto
2 tablespoons green pesto
1 cup grated Parmesan
½ cup finely grated cheddar
1 egg, beaten

makes about 24

1 Sprinkle a little flour on a clean work surface. Use a rolling pin to roll out the dough to a rectangle just over 20 x 10 inches. Using a large knife, trim the edges of the rectangle and then cut the pastry in half lengthwise to give 2 squares measuring roughly 10 x 10 inches.

2 Spread the red pesto over one square and green pesto over the other. Scatter some grated Parmesan and cheddar evenly over each square of pastry.

3 Take one square and fold the sides in toward the middle until they meet. Brush the top with a little beaten egg. Fold the sides in again to meet in the middle, then brush with more egg and fold in again. The pastry should now be in a long, thin roll. Place on a baking sheet and set aside while you do the same with the other square of pastry.

4 Chill the rolls in the fridge for 30 minutes.

5 Preheat the oven to 350°F.

6 Cut the pastry rolls into ⅜-inch slices and arrange the slices in a single layer on 2 baking sheets. Slightly flatten each palmier. **Ask an adult to help you** put one sheet on the middle shelf of the oven. Bake for about 20 minutes, or until golden and crisp.

7 Repeat to bake the second sheet of palmiers.

*Cheesy and just a little bit spicy,
these straws are nice with a mug
of Mulled Apple Juice (page 102).*

These nuts can be made well in advance and stored in an airtight container. Use unsalted and unroasted nuts from the baking section of the supermarket and feel free to vary the selection to include hazelnuts and walnuts if you prefer.

spiced mixed nuts

1⅓ **cups shelled Brazil nuts**
⅔ **cup shelled almonds**
⅔ **cup shelled pecans**
½ **teaspoon cayenne pepper**
½ **teaspoon ground cinnamon**
2 **tablespoons olive oil**
2 **teaspoons sugar**
½ **teaspoon sea salt flakes**
freshly ground black pepper

serves 6

1 Preheat the oven to 375°F.

2 Mix all the ingredients together well.

3 Spread evenly in a single layer on a baking sheet. **Ask an adult to help you** put the sheet on the middle shelf of the oven. Bake for about 10 minutes, or until golden and crisp.

4 Ask an adult to help you remove the sheet from the oven and let cool slightly before serving.

cheese straws

1 **cup all-purpose flour**
a pinch of sea salt
½ **teaspoon cayenne pepper**
½ **teaspoon mustard powder**
6½ **tablespoons unsalted butter, chilled and diced**
1 **cup mixed grated sharp cheddar and Parmesan**

a baking sheet, lined with baking parchment

makes about 24

1 Sift the flour, salt, cayenne, and mustard powder into the bowl of a food processor. Add the butter. **Ask an adult to help you** pulse the ingredients until they turn into crumbs.

2 Add the grated cheeses and pulse again until the dough starts to come together into a ball.

3 To knead the dough, sprinkle a little flour on a clean work surface. Shape the dough into a ball and push on it and press it onto the work surface. Do this briefly, just to bring the dough together. Flatten into a disc, cover with plastic wrap, and chill in the fridge for 30 minutes.

4 Preheat the oven to 375°F.

5 Tip the dough onto the floured work surface and roll out with a rolling pin until it is about ¼ inch thick. Cut into ⅜-inch wide strips and arrange on the prepared baking sheet.

6 Ask an adult to help you put the sheet on the middle shelf of the oven. Bake for about 12 minutes, or until golden.

7 Ask an adult to help you remove the sheet from the oven and let cool slightly before serving.

These knotted little bread rolls are so easy and delicious. They can be left plain or scattered with sesame seeds, poppy seeds, or grated cheese before baking. They're yummy with a bowl of Butternut Squash Soup (page 108).

pretzels

2⅓ cups bread flour

1 teaspoon sugar

1 teaspoon fast-acting
    dry yeast

½ teaspoon salt, plus
    extra for sprinkling

⅔ cup milk

1 tablespoon safflower oil

1 egg yolk, lightly beaten

1 tablespoon poppy seeds

1 tablespoon sesame seeds

*2 baking sheets, lined with
    baking parchment*

makes 8

1 Tip the flour, sugar, yeast, and salt into a large mixing bowl and make a hole like a well in the middle.

2 Put the milk in a small saucepan. **Ask an adult to help you** put the pan over low heat and heat up until the milk is warm. Stir the oil into the warm milk.

3 Pour the warm milk mixture into the well in the dry ingredients and mix with a wooden spoon until the ingredients come together into a dough.

4 To knead the dough, first sprinkle a little flour on a clean work surface. Then shape the dough into a ball and push on it and press it onto the work surface, turning it round often. You'll need to keep doing this until it is silky smooth and elastic—this will take about 8 minutes and you may need to add more flour if the dough is too sticky.

5 Shape the dough into a neat ball again. Wash and dry the mixing bowl and sit the dough back in it. Cover tightly with plastic wrap and leave in a warm place until the dough has doubled in size. This can take at least 1 hour.

6 Tip the dough onto the floured work surface and knead for 1 minute. Divide into 8 equal pieces. Roll each piece into a 16-inch long rope. Twist the dough rope into a knot and place on one of the prepared baking sheets.

7 Lightly oil a large sheet of plastic wrap, then use it to loosely cover the baking sheets (oiled-side down). Leave in a warm place to rise again for a further 30 minutes.

8 Preheat the oven to 375°F.

9 Gently brush the pretzels with the egg yolk and sprinkle with salt, poppy, or sesame seeds.

10 Ask an adult to help you put the baking sheets on the middle shelf of the preheated oven. Bake for 15 minutes, or until golden.

11 Ask an adult to help you remove the sheets from the oven and let cool for a few minutes before tipping out onto a wire rack.

index

A
Advent numbered cookies,
  66–7
almonds: almond crescents,
  39
  chocolate truffles, 32–3
  easy fruitcake, 94
  Lebkuchen, 16
  ricciarelli, 22
  rocky road fridge cake,
  52–3
  spiced mixed nuts, 123
apples: apple & cranberry
  pies, 59
  mulled apple juice, 102,
  122
  toffee apples, 31
avocado dip, 119

B
bagel chips, 118
baked Alaskas, mini, 86
basic recipes, 8–9
biscotti with pistachios &
  cranberries, 48
blueberries: frosted fruit, 74
  cranberry streusel muffins
  (*variation*), 28–9
  fruity treats, 89
Brazil nuts: spiced mixed
  nuts, 123
buttercream frosting, 9
buttermilk: buttermilk
  pancakes, 112–13
  cranberry streusel muffins,
  28–9
butternut squash soup with
  cheesy croutons, 108

C
cakes: basic yellow cake, 8
  bûche de Noël, 80
  coconut cake, 90
  easy fruitcake, 94
  Frosty the snowman, 97
  goodies for Santa &
  Rudolf, 56–7
  marble cake, 98–9

rocky road fridge cake,
  52–3
candy: candy trees, 72–3
  chocolate truffles, 32–3
  coconut ice, 27
  fudge, 34–5
  marshmallow pops, 20–1
  marshmallow snowmen,
  24–5
  peppermint creams, 18–19
cheese: butternut squash
  soup with cheesy
  croutons, 108
  cheese & ham scones,
  114–15
  cheese straws, 122, 123
  cheesy grissini, 107
  pesto palmiers, 120
chickpeas: red pepper &
  chickpea dip, 119
chocolate: bûche de Noël,
  80
  chocolate frosting, 9
  chocolate glaze, 8
  chocolate truffles, 32–3
  frosted brownie squares,
  12
  fudge, 34–5
  hot chocolate, 102, 103
  marble cake, 98–9
  marshmallow pops, 20–1
  mini baked Alaskas, 86
  pecan, toffee, & chocolate
  squares, 44
  rocky road fridge cake,
  52–3
  shortbread, 66
Christmas drinks: hot
  chocolate, 102
  mulled apple juice, 102,
  122
Christmas figures, marzipan,
  62–3
Christmas tree cookies, iced,
  40–1
cinnamon sticky buns, 50–1
coconut: coconut cake, 90
  coconut ice, 27

Frosty the snowman, 97
  marshmallow pops, 20–1
condensed milk: coconut
  ice, 27
  peppermint creams,
  18–19
cookies: Advent numbered
  cookies, 66–7
  almond crescents, 39
  biscotti with pistachios &
  cranberries, 48
  gingerbread shooting
  stars, 70
  goodies for Santa &
  Rudolf, 56–7
  iced Christmas tree
  cookies, 40–1
  Lebkuchen, 16
  ricciarelli, 22
  shortbread, 43
  snowflake cookies, 77
cranberries: apple &
  cranberry pies, 59
  biscotti with pistachios &
  cranberries, 48
  cranberry & pear relish,
  36–7
  cranberry streusel muffins,
  28–9
  frosted fruit, 74
  popcorn marshmallow
  clusters, 69
cream cheese & herb dip,
  119

D
dips, savory: avocado dip,
  119
  cream cheese & herb dip,
  119
  red pepper & chickpea
  dip, 119
dried fruit: apple &
  cranberry pies, 59
  biscotti with pistachios &
  cranberries, 48
  cranberry streusel muffins,
  28–9

easy fruitcake, 94
  fudge, 34–5
  popcorn marshmallow
  clusters, 69
  rocky road fridge cake,
  52–3
  Swedish saffron buns, 15
drinks, Christmas: hot
  chocolate, 102
  mulled apple juice, 102,
  122

EF
easy fruitcake, 56, 94
French toast, 110–11
fridge cake, rocky road,
  52–3
frosted fruit, 74
frosting: buttercream, 9
  chocolate, 9
  seven-minute, 90
Frosty the snowman, 97
fruit, frosted, 74
fruitcake, easy, 56, 94
fruity treats, 89
fudge, 34–5

G
gingerbread: gingerbread
  house, 84–5
  gingerbread shooting
  stars, 70
  goodies for Santa &
  Rudolf, 56–7
  Lebkuchen, 16
  pain d'épices, 83
glacé icing, 8
goodies for Santa & Rudolf,
  56–7
grapes: frosted fruit, 74
  fruity treats, 89
grissini, cheesy, 107

H
ham: cheese & ham scones,
  114–15
hazelnuts: almond crescents
  (*variation*), 39

chocolate truffles, 32–3
  rocky road fridge cake,
  52–3
honey: Lebkuchen, 16
  mulled apple juice, 102
  pain d'épices, 83
  rocky road fridge cake,
  52–3
hot chocolate, 102

IJ
ice cream: mini baked
  Alaskas, 86
iced Christmas tree cookies,
  40–1
icing: chocolate glaze, 8
  glacé, 8

LM
Lebkuchen, 16
madeleines, 47
maple syrup: buttermilk
  pancakes, 112–13
  French toast, 110–11
  pecan, toffee, & chocolate
  squares, 44
marble cake, 98–9
marshmallows: hot
  chocolate, 102
  marshmallow pops, 20–1
  marshmallow snowmen,
  24–5
  popcorn marshmallow
  clusters, 69
marzipan: goodies for Santa
  & Rudolf, 56–7
  marzipan Christmas
  figures, 62–3
meringue: meringue
  snowflakes, 55
mini baked Alaskas, 86
muffins, cranberry streusel,
  28–9
mulled apple juice, 102, 122

N
nuts: almond crescents, 39
  biscotti with pistachios &

conversion chart

cranberries, 48
chocolate truffles, 32–3
cinnamon sticky buns, 50–1
cranberry streusel muffins, 28–9
easy fruitcake, 94
frosted brownie squares, 12
Lebkuchen, 16
marshmallow pops, 20–1
pecan, toffee, & chocolate squares, 44
popcorn marshmallow clusters, 69
ricciarelli, 22
rocky road fridge cake, 52–3
spiced mixed nuts, 123
toffee apples, 31

P
pain d'épices, 83
palmiers, 120
pancakes: buttermilk pancakes, 112–13
Scotch pancakes with smoked salmon, 116
pears: cranberry & pear relish, 36–7
pecans: cinnamon sticky buns, 50–1
easy fruitcake, 94
frosted brownie squares, 12
pecan, toffee, & chocolate squares, 44
popcorn marshmallow clusters, 69
rocky road fridge cake, 52–3
spiced mixed nuts, 123
penguins, marzipan, 63
peppermint creams, 18–19
pesto palmiers, 120
pigs in blankets, 105
pistachios: biscotti with

pistachios & cranberries, 48
pomegranate: fruity treats, 89
popcorn: popcorn garlands, 68–9
popcorn marshmallow clusters, 69
pops, marshmallow, 20–1
pretzels, 124
pumpkin pie, 93

R
raisins: easy fruitcake, 94
fudge, 34–5
rocky road fridge cake, 52–3
Swedish saffron buns, 15
red pepper & chickpea dip, 119
reindeers, marzipan, 62
ricciarelli, 22
rocky road fridge cake, 52–3

S
saffron: Swedish saffron buns, 15
savory dips: avocado dip, 119
cream cheese & herb dip, 119
red pepper & chickpea dip, 119
scones: cheese & ham scones, 114–15
Scotch pancakes with smoked salmon, 116
seven-minute frosting, 90
shortbread, 43
Advent numbered cookies, 66–7
smoked salmon: Scotch pancakes with smoked salmon, 116
snowflake cookies, 77
snowflakes, meringue, 55
snowmen: Frosty the snowman, 97

marshmallow, 24–5
marzipan, 62
soup: butternut squash soup with cheesy croutons, 108
spiced mixed nuts, 123
sticky buns, cinnamon, 50–1
sugar mice, 65
Swedish saffron buns, 15

T
toffee: pecan, toffee, & chocolate squares, 44
toffee apples, 31
treats, fruity, 89

WY
walnuts: frosted brownie squares, 12
fudge, 34–5
rocky road fridge cake, 52–3
yellow cake, basic, 8

Weights and measures have been rounded up or down slightly to make measuring easier.

Measuring butter:
A US stick of butter weighs 4 oz. which is approximately 115 g or 8 tablespoons.

The recipes in this book require the following conversions:

American	Metric	Imperial
6 tbsp	85 g	3 oz.
7 tbsp	100 g	3½ oz.
1 stick	115 g	4 oz.

Volume equivalents:

American	Metric	Imperial
1 teaspoon	5 ml	
1 tablespoon	15 ml	
¼ cup	60 ml	2 fl. oz.
⅓ cup	75 ml	2½ fl. oz.
½ cup	125 ml	4 fl. oz.
⅔ cup	150 ml	5 fl. oz. (¼ pint)
¾ cup	175 ml	6 fl. oz.
1 cup	250 ml	8 fl. oz.

Weight equivalents:

Imperial	Metric
1 oz.	30 g
2 oz.	55 g
3 oz.	85 g
3½ oz.	100 g
4 oz.	115 g
6 oz.	175 g
8 oz. (½ lb.)	225 g
9 oz.	250 g
10 oz.	280 g
12 oz.	350 g
13 oz.	375 g
14 oz.	400 g
15 oz.	425 g
16 oz. (1 lb.)	450 g

Measurements:

Inches	cm
¼ inch	5 mm
½ inch	1 cm
1 inch	2.5 cm
2 inches	5 cm
3 inches	7 cm
4 inches	10 cm
5 inches	12 cm
6 inches	15 cm
7 inches	18 cm
8 inches	20 cm
9 inches	23 cm
10 inches	25 cm
11 inches	28 cm
12 inches	30 cm

Oven temperatures:

120°C	(250°F)	Gas ½
140°C	(275°F)	Gas 1
150°C	(300°F)	Gas 2
170°C	(325°F)	Gas 3
180°C	(350°F)	Gas 4
190°C	(375°F)	Gas 5
200°C	(400°F)	Gas 6
220°C	(425°F)	Gas 7

acknowledgments

I would like to say an enormous thank you to a few special people who have made this book so beautiful. To Lisa Linder for her fabulous pictures and to Liz Belton for her creative props and tableware—you are both a joy to work with! And to Céline and Megan at Ryland Peters & Small for putting the whole package together so wonderfully—as always.

And a big festive thank you to everyone who modeled, stirred, baked, and tasted on the photoshoots, and gave their seal of approval to the recipes.

And to Mungo, who sits patiently in his basket (on a good day) and waits until it's time for dinner and a long walk across the fields.

The publisher would like to thank the lovely models who appear in this book: Charlie; Constance and Lydia; Mackie; Thomas and Ollie; Celia, Max & Timmy; Polly and Will; Ella and Ben; Bella; Emma and Julian; Marly; Bluebelle; Imani and India; Malise; David; Saffron and Parisa.